Gilli Davies explores traditional Welsh country produce and cooking with some of Wales' best-loved recipes, with photographs by Huw Jones.

Flavours of Wales

GRAFFEG

I dedicate this book to my long suffering and supportive family. Work has occupied too much of my time.

However, being a cook has its benefits and I never stray far from the wise words of Oscar Wilde: 'After a good dinner, one can forgive anyone, even one's own relations!'

Gilli Davies

The Very Best Flavours of Wales first published by Gomer Press 1997. This new revised edition published by Graffeg 2011. Copyright © Graffeg 2011. ISBN 9781905582518

Flavours of Wales. Written by Gilli Davies. Photography © Huw Jones

Graffeg, Radnor Court, 256 Cowbridge Road East, Cardiff CF5 1GZ Wales UK. Tel: +44 (0)29 2078 5156 sales@graffeg.com www.graffeg.com

Graffeg are hereby identified as the authors of this work in accordance with section 77 of the Copyrights, Designs and Patents Act 1988.

Distributed by the Welsh Books Council www.cllc.org.uk castellbrychan@cllc.org.uk

A CIP Catalogue record for this book is available from the British Library.

Designed and produced by Peter Gill & Associates sales@petergill.com www.petergill.com

The publishers are also grateful to the Welsh Books Council for their financial support and marketing advice. www.gwales.com

Contents

The Flavours

Croeso i Gymru – Welcome to Wales – say the signs on the roadside, but what does a visitor expect to find on a Welsh menu?

Lamb, leeks, Caerphilly cheese and that healthy but extraordinary seaweed, laverbread, or perhaps a Welsh cake or slice of *bara brith*?

Our Celtic ancestors have left their imprint on Wales and there are similarities between Welsh fare and that prepared by our cousins in Scotland, Ireland and Brittany. The main feature of the early Welsh kitchen was the open-hearth fire and the bakestone or griddle, a flat piece of iron set over the fire, on which were cooked oatcakes and pancakes. Then there would be a large iron pot suspended above the fire. Boiling and stewing were the most important methods of cooking meat, and *cawl*. This all-in-one stew, once cooked over glowing embers, is still a popular dish. Today, you would be hard pressed to find a Welsh housewife who bakes her loaves daily, but take a trip to the old-fashioned, covered market in Swansea and you will be able to buy *bara planc*, bread cooked on a griddle, as well as crumbly, moist Welsh cakes.

Geraldus Cambrensis, the twelfth-century scholar who toured Wales in the company of Archbishop Baldwin in 1188, wrote in his journal:

Almost all the people live upon the produce of their herds, with oats, milk, cheese and butter.

The greater part of their land is laid down to pasturage; little is cultivated, a very small quantity is ornamented with flowers, and a still smaller is sown.

Wales was and, for the most part, still is a pastoral country and dairy farming remains important, especially in west Wales, from where, a mere 75 years ago, milk would be taken daily to London. Dairy produce, quickly made and sold at local markets, was a form of ready cash. Butter was made weekly and stored in casks, the milk would be left to stand so that the cream could be taken off the surface but, since churning took

# of Wales

place only once a week, the cream and resulting butter could have quite a strong flavour! The skimmed milk was fed to calves, but it was also used to make cheese. Prior to 1939 cheese was made on most farms but the Second World War put an end to production, and it wasn't until the introduction of milk quotas in the early 1980s that cheese was made again in Wales. Today, we have an enviable range: traditional Caerphilly, Cheddar-type cheeses, ewe's and goat's milk cheese, as well as smoked cheeses.

As for lamb: yes, it's good and so it should be! With a significant proportion of the farming population involved in the industry, we should be getting it right. Much lamb is exported and production is geared to overseas taste. For the most part the lamb is crossbred to produce lean meat and large lambs: lowland lamb from Easter on, then hill lamb from the end of August. I prefer hill lamb, noted for its succulent

flavour and firm texture, the product of slow maturing and a natural diet.

The production of natural or organic food in Wales is very much in vogue at this point in time. Indeed, we like to think that organic farming has its origins in Wales where it is now possible to buy organically produced meat, cheese, vegetables, fruit and dairy produce. Indeed, do look out for the roadside signs advertising cheese for sale, fresh baking,

home-made ice cream, goat's milk, fresh trout, Welsh honey, free-range poultry, local lobster and crab.

I can vouch for the quality of all the raw ingredients available but, if you are in any doubt, then why not visit one of the many excellent hotels or guest houses in Wales, where the good cooking of local produce comes naturally, in order to experience the very best flavours of Wales.

In a moment the kitchen was full. All the girls ran round the back lane and through the back door, and processions came and went through the front, all taking out plates of bread and butter and pies and cakes and buckets and baths of hot water for the teapots, all getting in each other's way and laughing and pushing and pretending to be stuck in the doorway.

My mother came through the crowd with a big blackberry tart in one hand and my tea in the other, carrying them high and with care not to spill, keeping off the people with her elbows and eyes.

Richard Llewellyn, *How Green Was My Valley* (1939).

Cawl

Bacon Cawl with Vegetables

1

Cawl

Cawl, pronounced 'cowl', is the Welsh word for soup, and today it generally refers to the classic, peasant soup or stew. Mention *cawl* to anyone in Wales and they will tell you about a hearty dish consisting of meat and vegetables, similar to a *pot au feu*.

In north Wales it is called *lobsgows*, meaning 'soup for the scawsers', or those people who came from Liverpool.

Cawl dates back to the Celtic kitchen. Just imagine a cauldron of *cawl* suspended over the embers of a large open fire. Originally, the meat would be lifted out of the vegetable broth and eaten first, the soup being enjoyed the following day. Served in small wooden bowls and eaten with wooden spoons so that it wouldn't burn the mouth, *cawl*, at one time, was the staple diet of many Welsh households.

Ask any Welsh housewife for her *cawl* recipe and it will undoubtedly differ from that of her neighbours. Some Welsh cooks opt for pork or bacon, others prefer lamb or beef, the meat included dependent on what is most readily available. As for vegetables, potatoes and a mixture of root vegetables, such as carrots, swede and turnip, usually find their way into *cawl*. The most important thing to remember is to prepare well in advance, because making *cawl* is a two (if not three) day job.

Today, *cawl* is part of a balanced diet, a satisfying meal that people enjoy from time to time, but particularly on a cold winter's day. However, it is not so long ago that almost every meal in rural Wales included *cawl* in some form or other. Fresh herbs, often winter savory, was grown near the back door so that it could easily be picked and added to the *cawl*. Only salted meat would have been available, and oatmeal, mixed with a little water and stirred in, was added to the *cawl* to make it go further. Sometimes, cooked oatcakes were crushed and added to a bowl of *cawl* that had been reheated three or four times, and served at breakfast time. In cold weather, *cawl* would be followed by apple or plain dumplings, made by mixing flour with a spoonful of *cawl* to form a thick paste. The paste was then spread around an unskinned apple and left to simmer on top of the soup.

Leeks are traditionally added to *cawl* shortly before serving, to add flavour and also decoration. Another way to brighten up a bowl of *cawl* and add a dash of colour was to sprinkle marigold petals over the steaming bowls before serving. If marigolds were out of season, then the cook made do with mashed carrot.

Nan's Cawl

This recipe was given to me by Nan Humphreys who ran Penbontbren Hotel, a restaurant and farm holiday business situated about 10 miles north-east of Cardigan. Nan based most of the dishes served in her restaurant on traditional Welsh recipes and all the ingredients used were locally obtained, if at all possible. This recipe for *cawl* is the one her mother would prepare for her as a child.

Ingredients

For the stock

a piece of brisket

a bunch of fresh herbs

salt and pepper

For the soup

2 potatoes

½ swede

1 large or 2 small turnips

3 carrots

2 parsnips

a couple of sticks of celery

2 – 3 leeks, depending on size

optional – chopped parsley, finely chopped savoy cabbage or shredded sprouts

Serves 4 – 6

1 On the first day, make the stock.

2 Cover the brisket of beef with cold water, add the herbs and seasoning and bring to the boil.

3 Cover with a lid and simmer the beef very gently for at least 2 hours. Leave the beef to cool in the liquid overnight.

4 Next day, skim the fat from the surface of the stock and remove the brisket to serve at another time, possibly after the cawl.

5 Peel and dice all the root vegetables, slice the celery and add all the vegetables to the stock.

6 Bring to the boil and simmer gently for 20 – 30 minutes.

7 Wash and finely chop the leeks, both green and white parts, add to the soup and simmer for a further 15 – 20 minutes. (Add any of the optional ingredients at this stage too.)

8 Serve the cawl with wholemeal bread or rolls and pieces of Caerphilly cheese.

9 If there is any left over, then heat it up the next day. This is when it tastes at its very best.

Bacon Cawl with Vegetables

In the past, a pot of *cawl* might have been made from bacon that had been hanging on a hook in the kitchen to cure during the cold winter months. With root vegetables and herbs from the garden, there's nothing quite like a steaming bowl of *cawl* on a cold day.

1 Soak the bacon or ham overnight in cold water to remove some of the salt.

2 Rinse well and place in a large pan with enough cold water to cover.

3 Add the onion, carrot, parsnip, bay leaf and parsley stalks.

4 Simmer gently for an hour, then leave to cool before skimming the fat from the surface.

5 Remove the bacon from the stock, strain the liquor and retain for later.

6 Remove some bacon slices and set aside for another meal, before cutting the remainder into chunks for the *cawl*.

7 Gently fry the cubed carrots, parsnips, turnips and the white portion of the leek in 25g (1oz) of butter.

8 Pour on the reserved stock, add the chunks of bacon and the chopped parsley, savory and green leek.

9 Simmer for a further 20 minutes.

10 Season well and serve the *cawl* with chunks of fresh bread.

11 Alternatively, leave overnight for the flavours to develop.

Ingredients

1kg (2lbs) piece of bacon or ham, shoulder or corner

1 onion, cut in half

1 carrot

1 parsnip

1 bay leaf

a bunch of parsley, stems and tops used separately

1 large leek, white and green part separated and diced

3 carrots, peeled and cubed

2 parsnips, peeled and cubed

2 turnips, peeled and cubed

a bunch of fresh winter savory or sage

salt and pepper

Serves 4 – 6

Lobsgows

I received this recipe from Dilys Hughes, who was based at the tea-room in Llynnon Mill, Llanddeusant, Anglesey. Dilys maintains that 'It's a matter of personal taste what you include in *lobsgows*.'

Ingredients

450g (1lb) chuck steak, cut into 1 inch squares

marrow bone

3 medium onions, sliced

2 large carrots, scraped and cut into large chunks

1 small swede, peeled and cut into chunks

3 large potatoes, peeled and diced

2 medium leeks, washed and diced

1.2 litres (2 pints) hot water

salt and freshly milled black pepper

Serves 4

1 Simmer the steak, marrow bone and onions in 1.2 litres (2 pints) of water for about 1½ hours.

2 Add seasoning and the prepared vegetables, and simmer for a further hour.

3 Correct the seasoning and serve on a cold winter's day with plenty of fresh, crusty bread.

Spiced Leek and Potato Soup

In the case of this recipe, the combination of leeks and potatoes is used to make either a warming winter soup or a sophisticated chilled soup for a hot summer's day.

1 Melt the butter in a medium-sized saucepan and fry the vegetables with the curry paste and coriander seeds for 3 – 4 minutes, until they begin to soften.

2 Add the chicken stock and bring to the boil.

3 Cover and simmer for 30 minutes, or until the vegetables are soft.

4 Puree the soup and sieve for a really fine texture.

5 Adjust the seasoning and either serve piping hot or cover and chill for 2 hours, preferably overnight.

6 Before serving, swirl the cream on top of the soup as a garnish with the fresh coriander.

Ingredients

25g (1oz) butter

4 medium-size leeks, trimmed, washed and chopped

2 medium-sized potatoes, peeled and chopped

1 teaspoon mild curry paste

1 teaspoon coriander seeds, freshly ground

600ml (1 pint) chicken stock

4 tablespoons single cream

coriander leaves, freshly chopped

Serves 4

When we sat down, with me in Mama's lap, my father would ladle out of the cauldron thin leek soup with a big lump of ham in it, that showed its rind as it turned over through the steam when the ladle came out brimming over. There was a smell with that soup. It is in my nostrils now. There was everything in it that was good, and because of that, the smell alone was enough to make you feel so warm and comfortable it was a pleasure to be sitting there, for you knew of the pleasure to come.

Richard Llewellyn, *How Green Was My Valley* (1939).

Cockles and other Shellfish

Warm Cockle Salad

2

Cockles and other Shellfish

South Walians are still passionately fond of cockles.

Indeed, they have been enjoyed over the centuries, for their empty shells have been found at many historical sites, including caves – the home of prehistoric man – Roman forts and castles. At one time, cockles were gathered along the West Coast but today the largest stocks are to be found in Carmarthen Bay. Since the Middle Ages, cockles and other locally-gathered produce have played an important part in the economy of the north Gower coast. For centuries, Gower women would walk barefoot as far as the outskirts of Swansea, then wash their feet at Olchfa (literally, 'the washing place') before putting on their boots to enter the town in order to sell their wares in the market.

Indeed, freshly cooked cockles are still sold in Swansea Market, and from vans and market stalls throughout south Wales.

Until the late 1940s, the north Gower cockle industry, centered upon Penclawdd, was almost exclusively the preserve of women. Today, there are some 50 gatherers operating within the Burry Estuary with ten family-run, cockle-producing factories situated along the north Gower coast. The gathering itself is a back-breaking occupation. Working at low tide, groups head for the sands armed with a rake (known as a cram) and a scraper or scrap. Bending from the waist, the gatherers scoop the cockles from just below the surface of the sand into a sieve or riddle, which is shaken hard so as to separate the larger from the smaller cockles; the latter discarded to grow bigger. Whereas once they gathered with the aid of a horse and cart, tractors are now permitted to carry the heavy sacks across the vast expanse of sand exposed at low tide. As soon as they reach the factory, the cockles are steam cooked, which opens the shells, and in the process of rinsing, the meat separates from the shells. Then it's off to market, or further afield. The cockle-gathering families who once carried baskets of their freshly-cooked shellfish from door-to-door in the industrial valleys of south Wales now sell their cockle meat worldwide.

Some of the tastiest ways to eat cockles

If you visit Fairyhill, a country hotel at Reynoldston on the Gower peninsula, a bowl of crispy fried cockles will accompany your drinks at the bar. They are quite the best appetiser I know. Take a handful of fresh cockles, squeeze gently to remove all excess moisture, season well, toss in plain flour and deep fry in very hot oil for about 6 – 7 minutes. Serve immediately. A favourite way of serving cockles in Penclawdd is to fry them with a little onion, bacon, parsley and breadcrumbs. Serve straight from the pan. Cockles may also be eaten freshly boiled and sprinkled with pepper.

Tips on Shellfish

There is good reason for the old adage, 'Only eat shellfish if there is an "r" in the month'. Although eating shellfish during the summer months (that is, when there is no 'r' in the month) will do you no harm, shellfish generally spawn during the warm months of May, June, July and August, and their flesh is much less good to eat. Today, all shellfish are treated in purification units but do heed the following advice:

Before cooking, discard any shells that are open and after cooking discard any shells that remain shut.

Gower Cockle

and Bacon Pie

Ingredients

450g (1lb) lean smoked bacon, cut into fine strips

1 large onion, peeled and chopped

50g (2oz) butter

50g (2oz) flour

600ml (1 pint) milk

450g (1lb) freshly cooked cockles

1 tablespoon chopped chives

1 tablespoon chopped parsley

100ml (4fl oz) dry white wine

salt and freshly ground black pepper

For the pie topping

450g (1lb) potatoes, peeled and boiled

1 small leek, finely grated

25g (1oz) butter, melted

salt and freshly ground black pepper

2oz (50g) strong Cheddar cheese, grated

Serves 4

1 In a medium-sized saucepan, gently fry the bacon strips and onion in the butter for 5 minutes.

2 Stir in the flour and cook for another minute, but do not brown. Gradually add the milk, stirring continuously and bring to the boil.

3 Add the cockles, chives, parsley, wine and seasoning. Pour into a 1.2 litre (2 pint) pie dish.

4 For the topping, mash the potatoes with the leek, add the melted butter and seasoning, and spread the potato mixture over the cockles and sauce.

5 Sprinkle the grated cheese over the top and bake for 30 minutes in a medium oven until golden-brown and crisp.

Sprinkle the grated cheese over the top and bake for 30 minutes in a medium oven until golden-brown and crisp.

Warm Cockle Salad

1 Arrange the salad leaves on four plates ready to serve.

2 In a large frying pan or skillet, heat the sunflower oil and fry the mushrooms for one minute.

3 Then toss in the cockles, ham and nuts and continue frying, stirring all the time for another minute.

4 Add the walnut oil and vinegar and immediately pour the contents of the pan over the four plates of salad leaves, dividing the sauce evenly.

5 Serve at once with warm rolls. Home-made walnut rolls taste wonderful with this dish!

Serve at once with warm rolls. Home-made walnut rolls taste wonderful with this dish!

Ingredients

This is a recipe I created for the Swansea Cockle Festival.

225g (8oz) cockles

225g (8oz) mushrooms, as many varieties as possible, sliced

100g (4oz) Carmarthen Ham or any other air-dried ham, cut into snippets

50g (2oz) walnuts, broken into pieces

1 tablespoon sunflower or vegetable oil

2 tablespoons walnut oil

2 tablespoons cider or white wine vinegar

mixed salad leaves

Serves 4

Scallops, particularly the small queen scallops, are plentiful in Cardigan Bay, and have been landed on Anglesey for generations. Recipes from the past describe how their pretty little shells were used to shape shortbread biscuits, called Berffro Cakes, made in Aberffraw on the west coast of Anglesey. Originally they were called Cacennau Iago, after the pilgrim, Saint James, whose motif is the scallop shell. The queen scallop is a different species to the more common king scallop. The shell, about half the size of a king scallop, is approximately 6cm (2½ inches) across, and the nuggets of flesh inside are about the size of a small walnut. Scallops filter feed on the sea bed and, in an ideal world, are hand-picked by divers. In reality, however, dredging is the most successful method of harvesting. Rather like a giant crab, a trawler lowers two nets into the sea and scoops up the scallops off the sea bed. Following their temporary storage on-board ship, the molluscs are unloaded and put into sacks on the quayside prior to being taken to a processing plant. Here they are set upon by a bevy of women who attack them with sharp-bladed knives used to prise open the shells with a swift flick of the wrist. After being briefly tumbled in fresh water to wash away grains of sand, the scallops are ready for packing or freezing. Many are sold fresh, but a small, thriving industry is involved in the export of scallops to France.

Scallops

Queenie Scallops
with Laverbread

Chefs are always keen to buy these tiny, delicious molluscs, although cooking them is something of an art. Overcook a scallop and you will ruin the delicate flavour and fine tenderness. Just a few seconds in a hot pan is all that is required. And take care of the bright red coral, or roe, for this needs even less cooking. Scallops are best in spring and autumn.

1 Clean the scallops and dry on kitchen paper. Leave the corals attached wherever possible.

2 In a large frying pan, heat the butter until it sizzles.

3 Toss in half the scallops and fry quickly so that they cook on all sides.

4 Remove from the pan, as soon as possible, and keep warm in six individual serving dishes.

5 Place the laverbread in the pan with the orange rind and wine, bring to the boil, taste for seasoning and add the cream or *crème fraîche*.

6 Pour the sauce over the scallops and serve immediately.

7 Serve with fresh herb rolls or warm herb bread.

Ingredients

450g (1lb) queen scallops

25g (1oz) butter

1 tablespoon laverbread (pulped spinach as an alternative)

½ grated orange rind

1 glass dry white wine (Welsh, if possible)

1 tablespoon double cream or *crème fraîche*.

As a starter to serve 6

Mussels have been gathered in Wales for generations, their shells, together with cockles, having been unearthed at a number of prehistoric and Roman sites. Remarkably, the method of gathering has changed little; hand-pickers still operate in Carmarthen Bay and along the shores of the Gower peninsula, whilst a very simple dredging system is in operation in the Conwy Estuary. During the 19th century Conwy mussels were famous for their pearls.

The waters around Penrhyn Castle, near Bangor, and the Menai Straits have been seeded with mussels, where a larger dredging operation takes place.

The mussel-gathering season lasts from September to May. During the summer months, however, they are not at their best for when spawning they have very little edible flesh.

Mussels

Spicy Mussel Casserole

This is one of my favourite winter-warming dishes. It is quick, easy to make and full of brilliant colour.

1. Prepare slices of toasted French bread, rubbed with halved cloves of garlic and generously dusted with fresh chopped parsley.

2. Combine the onion, garlic, stock, vinegar and chillies in a large pan.

3. Cover and bring to the boil. Boil for 5 – 7 minutes.

4. Uncover, lower the heat and simmer until the onions are tender and the liquid has almost gone.

5. Stir in the herbs, cook for a minute, then add the tomatoes and simmer for 15 minutes.

6. Add the fish and mussels, and season to taste.

7. Simmer for 5 – 7 minutes until the fish is cooked through and the mussels open.

8. Place a slice of toast in a shallow soup dish, ladle the fish and sauce over the toast and sprinkle with parsley.

Ingredients

1 large onion, sliced

2 cloves garlic, crushed

300ml (½ pint) fish, chicken or vegetable stock

3 tablespoons balsamic vinegar

¼ teaspoon crushed red chillies

½ tablespoon fresh rosemary, finely chopped

3 tablespoons fresh parsley, finely chopped

two 400g (14oz) tins chopped tomatoes

375g (12oz) fillet of cod cut into 2.5cm (1 inch) cubes

18 – 24 well scrubbed mussels

salt and freshly ground pepper to taste

Serves 4

Ladle the fish and sauce over the toast and sprinkle with parsley.

Although there are still a great many lobsters in the waters off the west coast of Wales, large numbers are now sent to France and Spain in lorries full of seawater where they command a higher price. Nevertheless, it is still possible to find fresh crab on the menu of many a small restaurant along the Welsh coast. Lobsters and crabs have for centuries been caught along the shores of the Llŷn peninsula, but in all probability they only became part of the rural economy of the Cardigan Bay coast during the last century.

George Owen, the Elizabethan historian and author of *The Description of Pembrokeshire* (1603), claimed that the lobsters caught off the coast of Pembrokeshire were 'very sweet and delicate meat and plenty taken'.

Spend a little time in any of the small harbours along the west coast of Wales and you will see lobster pots being brought ashore or despatched to sea aboard small fishing vessels.

Lobster and Crab

Porthgain Crab

in Mild Llanboidy Cheese Sauce

This recipe was given to me by Annie Davies, at the Harbour Lights Restaurant in Porthgain.

1 Boil the fresh crab in salted water for approximately 20 minutes.

2 Pour the milk into a saucepan, add the celery, bay leaf, parsley, black pepper, and onion studded with the cloves.

3 Heat gently and, just before it boils, remove from the heat and leave to infuse for about 30 minutes.

4 In another pan, melt the butter, stir in the flour and cook for a minute.

5 Pour in the strained, flavoured milk and stir until it thickens. Add the cream and 50g (2oz) of Llanboidy cheese.

6 Season to taste. Spread a little of the crab meat on the bottom of the upturned, cleaned crab shells.

7 Season and cover with the sauce, top with the rest of the cheese and bake for 10 – 15 minutes in a moderate oven (400°F [200°C], Gas 6) and brown under the grill.

Ingredients

4 fresh, medium-sized crabs (or dressed crab), allowing 125g (6oz) per person

100g (4oz) white and 50g (2oz) brown meat

150ml (5fl oz) milk

1 stick of celery

1 bay leaf

3 sprigs of parsley

6 black peppercorns

½ onion

3 cloves

50g (2oz) butter

50g (2oz) flour

50ml (2fl oz) cream

175g (6oz) Llanboidy or mature Cheddar cheese

Serves 6 – 8 as a first course, 4 as a main course

Oysters Gratinée

At the beginning of the last century, oysters were sold for as little as a penny a dozen, so plentiful were they in the estuaries of south-west Wales. Popular with the Romans, they became the basis of a nourishing industry during the Middle Ages and by the beginning of the 18th century were dredged on a large scale near Oystermouth, on the shores of Swansea Bay. Alas, those oyster beds are now barren but new stocks of Pacific oysters are being farmed in the Menai Straits in north Wales. Upwards of three million little oysters have been placed on wooden trays, set in the fast flowing water of the Menai Straits, and in time these will grow into the delicacies we so much appreciate.

Ingredients

12 oysters

100g (4oz) pulped laverbread

150ml (¼ pint) double cream

100g (4oz) Caerphilly cheese

crumbled pinch of nutmeg and freshly ground black pepper

50g (2oz) fresh, brown breadcrumbs

Serves 4

1 Spread the laverbread over the bottom of four shallow dishes.

2 Arrange the oysters on top, three to each dish.

3 Mix the cream with the cheese, nutmeg and pepper and pour over the oysters.

4 Sprinkle over the breadcrumbs.

5 Pop under a moderate grill for 10 minutes until bubbling and golden brown on top.

Crab and Cockle Fishcakes

with Bloody Mary Sauce

To this splendid fishcake recipe from Nant Ddu Lodge, north of Merthyr Tydfil on the A470, I have added a devilishly good sauce!

1 Thoroughly mix all of the ingredients.

2 Divide into small patties and place on a tray.

3 Chill for half an hour. Then flour, egg and breadcrumb each cake and shallow fry in oil until golden brown.

4 Mix all the ingredients for the sauce together and pour over the fishcakes.

Ingredients

275g (10oz) crab meat and cockles (mixed as you wish)

175g (6oz) fresh, white breadcrumbs

1 teaspoon cajun spices

1 tablespoon mayonnaise

2 sprigs fresh basil

For the coating and frying

plain flour

beaten egg

fresh breadcrumbs

vegetable oil

Bloody Mary Sauce

300ml (½ pint) tomato pulp or puree

2 tablespoons vodka

1 teaspoon Worcester sauce

good squeeze of lemon juice

Serves 4 – 6

And the crab does sensibly feel the course of the moon, and filling and emptying itself with the increase and decrease thereof, and therefore is said to be best at the full moon.

George Owen, *The Description of Pembrokeshire* (1603).

Scallop and Prawn Kebabs

with Lime Dill Butter Sauce

There is more to a good barbecue than meets the eye – so often the meal is expected to cook itself with the help of a gusting wind and flaming charcoal. So, lesson number one is to appoint a cook! Give the cook a drink, settle the person down beside the barbecue and tell him or her that the meal depends on their attention. Grilling tends to dry ingredients, so, whatever you choose to barbecue, it is a wise precaution to marinade first, then brush with oil whilst cooking. Also, have a dish ready into which you can place the cooked food so that it doesn't linger too long on the barbecue.

1 Take two of the limes, grate the rind and squeeze the juice.

2 Place into a dish with the chopped chilli and oil, and season with salt and pepper.

3 Trim the scallops, cut the white fish into 2.5cm (1 inch) cubes and place into the dish with the prawns.

4 Toss in the marinade, then cover and refrigerate for half an hour.

5 Cut the remaining limes into wedges and arrange on 8 skewers with the fish.

6 Brush with oil and cook over hot coals for 6 – 8 minutes, turning once and brushing with the marinade.

Ingredients

8 prawns

450g (1lb) queen scallops

375g (12oz) firm, white fish; for example, monkfish, cod or haddock

4 limes

1 small green chilli, de-seeded and finely chopped

2 tablespoons oil

salt and freshly ground black pepper

1 Place the egg yolks into a bowl and whisk in the lime rind and juice.

2 Place over a pan of simmering water and gradually whisk in the butter.

3 Continue to whisk until the sauce thickens.

4 Remove from the pan and add the dill.

5 Serve while still warm with seafood kebabs.

Lime Dill Butter

2 egg yolks

grated rind of 1 lime and 1 tablespoon lime juice

100g (4oz) butter

2 tablespoons chopped dill

Serves 4

Lesson number one is to appoint a cook!

Laverbread

Speckled Seaweed Pie

3

Laverbread, a cooked seaweed, is enjoyed by the Welsh, particularly in south Wales. Its Latin name is *Porphyra umbilicalis* and because of its popularity, it has been called *Welshman's Caviar*.

Over past centuries laver has been gathered in various parts of the British Isles, particularly in Ireland and Scotland where it is known as *sloke* or kelp.

Gathering laver is no fun. It must be plucked off the rocks of the Gower and Pembrokeshire coast at low tide, and it should come as no surprise that candidates for this cold, unpleasant job are easier to find during the summer rather than the winter months. But each gatherer is reluctant to divulge his source of supply to his friends. Indeed, so fickle is this seaweed that it rarely appears two years running in the same place, and often disappears for several years. Once gathered, it requires much washing, for sand loves to stick to it. Then it must be boiled – some say for at least seven hours – but if the laver is soft and fresh, less time is required. Once soft, the laver is chopped or pureed. There are still some dedicated cooks in west Wales who collect and pulp their own laver, and the resulting laverbread has a coarser texture and a more distinctive flavour than the commercially processed, greenish-black pulp.

Just as it has for the past century, laver is still processed in Penclawdd, alongside the cockle-cooking plants. But with diminishing supplies around the Welsh coast, much of the laver now arrives from Scotland. It is washed, washed and washed again, before being boiled for at least seven hours in large containers. The smell, and oozing, gelatinous green slime that is the by-product of the process, is remarkable; some people love it, but some hate it. Finally, the weed is pulped until smooth, and pureed before being despatched to the markets.

Swansea Market is still the main outlet for laverbread. It is sold on the cockle stands, wrapped in clear cellophane, with or without a dusting of oatmeal. Housewives either mix it with extra oatmeal to form little cakes for frying or just heat it through in a frying pan containing bacon fat, before spreading it over fried bread.

Fashionable chefs in Wales are also seriously interested in this 'unknown ingredient from the sea'. From Anglesey to Monmouthshire, cooks are demanding supplies of cooked seaweed to add flavour and

Laverbread

regional distinctiveness to their dishes.

Over the past few years laver has also become something of a 'hero' ingredient with Japanese visitors who have heard about it at home. They often arrive in Wales with the sole intention of tasting Welsh laverbread. But they are intrigued to find it in such a gooey state, because the very same seaweed is grown and cultivated on the shores of Japan, where it is dried in sheets and called *nori*.

Laverbread combines well with any fish or shellfish dish, makes a good glutinous filling or stuffing, is a fine additional ingredient in soup, and when combined with sharp orange or lemon juice and a knob of butter, makes an interesting sauce for lamb.

Its health-giving properties are well known, and during the 18th century laverbread was eaten by those taking the waters at Bath Spa. Laver is extremely nutritious because it contains a high proportion of protein, iodine and vitamins B, B2, A, D and C. It also contains very few calories. Its popularity in south Wales may have something to do with the fact that it was a particularly healthy component in the diet of coal miners.

Even today laverbread is taken up to the valleys, together with cockles and other shellfish, on a weekly basis. Not so long ago it was sold from door-to-door around Swansea and Llanelli by women carrying the little paper-wrapped, shilling packages of laver in huge, wicker baskets.

But how did it get its name? I think that it may simply be from the Welsh, *bara lawr*, which translates literally as 'bread of the floor', a staple ingredient for those who wish to bend down and pluck it!

Deep-fried Laver Seaweed

Here is a speciality that Franco and Ann Taruschio served to visitors to nibble as they sat in the bar at The Walnut Tree, Llanddewi Skirrid, near Abergavenny.

Ingredients

100g (4oz) laver seaweed

flour

vegetable oil for deep-frying

roasted Szechuan pepper

ground coriander seed

Serves 4

1 Wash the laver seaweed thoroughly to remove the sand.

2 Leave the seaweed to drain in a colander and then dry thoroughly.

3 Tear the laver into strips, dip in flour and shake off the excess. Deep-fry the laver for about 2 – 3 minutes until crisp.

4 Sprinkle with ground-roasted Szechuan pepper, coriander and salt. Serve as a nibble with drinks.

5 To make roasted Szechuan pepper, dry-fry the pepper until a strong aromatic perfume is given off, then grind in a spice grinder.

6 A spice grinder is an absolute must in the kitchen, as previously ground spice does not have the same aroma and taste.

In 1877 the celebrated Victorian critic Eneas Dallas complained that laver had lost its popularity and was no longer served in London clubs. He wrote thus:

If only French cooks had ruled England they would have made it as famous as the truffles of Perigord.

A Welsh Breakfast

1 Gently fry some dry-cured bacon so that the fat runs and flavours the pan.

2 Remove the bacon from the pan and keep warm while you fry the laver cakes in the bacon fat.

3 Add these to the bacon and keep warm, before cooking the cockles and eggs in the remnants of the bacon juices. Serve at once.

Cockles and Eggs

1 Fry the cockles in a little bacon fat for a few minutes, then pour over the beaten eggs.

2 Stir well with a wooden spoon until the egg is lightly cooked.

3 Season with pepper.

Ingredients

175g (6oz) freshly cooked cockles, out of shell

2 eggs, beaten

freshly milled black pepper

Laver Cakes

1 Mix the laverbread and the oatmeal and shape into little rissole-like cakes about 5cm (2 inches) across and 2cm (¾ inch) thick.

2 Slide the laver cakes into the hot bacon fat and fry fairly quickly for 2 – 3 minutes on each side, shaping and patting the cakes with a palette knife as they fry. Lift out carefully.

Ingredients

100g (4oz) fresh or tinned laverbread

25g (1oz) medium or fine oatmeal

Serves 4

Mousseline of Scallop, Crab and Laverbread

with Crab Sauce

This recipe was given to me by Chris Chown of Plas Bodegroes for the *Tastes of Wales* TV Series. It is quite complicated but well worth the effort.

Ingredients

450g (1lb) hen crab

1cm (½ inch) fresh ginger, finely chopped

salt and pepper

1 small onion

½ stick celery

1 clove garlic

25g (1oz) butter

50 ml (2fl oz) medium sherry

1 teaspoon tomato puree

1 bay leaf

Serves 4

1 Boil the crab for 10 minutes in salted water, then cool quickly.

2 Discard the stomach and dead man's fingers.

3 Remove all the flesh.

4 Mix half the brown meat with the white meat and ginger.

5 Season and reserve.

6 Smash the crab shell and place in a saucepan.

7 Add the chopped onion, celery and garlic, and butter and sweat until they begin to brown.

8 Add the sherry, the tomato puree and bay leaf; cover the pan for a minute.

9 Pour in 600ml (1 pint) water and simmer for 1 hour.

It is quite complicated but well worth the effort.

1 Keep 24 of the scallops for garnish.

2 Detach the roes from the remaining scallops and reserve. Place the remaining chilled, white scallop meat (approx. 250g [9oz]) in a food processor bowl and sprinkle with a little salt.

3 Add the egg, and puree for 60 seconds, gradually adding three-quarters of the well-chilled cream.

4 Rub through a fine sieve.

5 Add pepper.

6 Poach a small amount in simmering water to test consistency; if it is very firm, add a little more chilled cream.

7 Test again until it is light. (Remember, laverbread is very salty.)

8 Butter eight 120ml (4fl oz) timbale moulds or ramekins.

9 Divide the mousse between them and form a well in the centre of each.

10 Place a teaspoonful of laverbread and then a teaspoonful of the reserved mixed crabmeat in each.

11 Push in the scallop roes and chill.

For the mousse

450g (1lb) freshly shelled queen scallop meat, or 3kg (7lbs) queen scallops in shells

salt and pepper

1 egg

200ml (7fl oz) double cream, chilled

100g (4oz) laverbread

---

1 Strain the stock into a clean pan; add the wine and cream and reduce the quantity by half.

2 Add the reserved brown crab meat and sherry.

3 Boil briefly and sieve into a clean pan. Whisk in the butter and re-heat, checking seasoning.

4 Steam the mousselines for 8 minutes or cook in a *bain-marie* for 8 – 12 minutes until slightly risen and firm.

5 Turn out the mousselines and surround with sauce.

6 Garnish with three sautéed scallops.

For the sauce

100ml (3½fl oz) white wine

100ml (3½fl oz) double cream

25ml (1fl oz) medium sherry

50g (2oz) butter

seasoning

Speckled Seaweed Pie

A recipe by Debbie Cumming of the Catering Department, University of Wales Institute, Cardiff.

Ingredients

Pastry

100g (4oz) flour

50g (2oz) butter or lard

25g (1oz) laverbread

30ml (2 tablespoons) water

salt

1 Sieve the flour and salt together.

2 Rub the fat lightly into the flour until the mixture resembles fine, even breadcrumbs.

3 Stir in 25g (1oz) of the laverbread and the water, mixing to form a dough.

4 Leave to rest for a few minutes before rolling out.

5 Lightly grease a 22cm (9 inch) flan dish and line with pastry.

6 Bake blind by placing a round of greaseproof paper inside the dish and arrange baking beans evenly over the bottom. Bake at 400°F (200°C), Gas 6 for 10 minutes.

Filling

25g (1oz) butter

2 rashers bacon, chopped

1 clove garlic, crushed

225g (8oz) cooked cockles

2 eggs

90ml (3fl oz) milk

60ml (2fl oz) double cream

225g (8oz) ricotta cheese

50g (2oz) laverbread

Serves 4

1 Heat the butter in a pan, add the bacon and garlic, and fry gently for 5 minutes.

2 Line the pastry case with the cockles, bacon and garlic.

3 Whisk the eggs, milk and cream together and add seasoning.

4 Blend in the ricotta cheese and laverbread, and pour the mixture into the pastry case.

5 Bake at 400°F (200°C), Gas 6 for 30 – 35 minutes.

6 After baking, garnish with a sprig of parsley.

7 The pie can be served hot or cold.

Noisettes of Lamb

with Laver and Orange Sauce

As today, great emphasis was placed on the origin of ingredients in the 19th century. Londoners loved to eat mountain lamb from Wales, which they perceived to be the best available. Lamb grazed on the marshlands around Romney on the south-east coast of England was also famous for its salty tang. Naturally, a sauce made from local ingredients would also have been popular.
To quote Collins, 1875: 'A capital dinner! You don't get marsh mutton with hot laver sauce every day!'

Fresh or tinned laverbread works well with this sauce but if neither are available, try pulped spinach with a good dash of anchovy essence.

1 In a small pan, heat the laverbread and fruit juice.

2 Cook for a few minutes, stirring all the time.

3 Add the butter little by little until the sauce looks rich and glossy.

4 Add enough lamb stock to ensure a good pouring consistency.

5 Season to taste and keep warm.

6 Heat the grill to its hottest and cook the noisettes, turning once, until they are crisp on the outside but still a little pink in the middle.

7 Serve the lamb with the sauce separately, with a potch of mashed root vegetables, such as carrot and parsnip or swede, to offset the richness of the laver sauce.

Ingredients

225g (8oz) laverbread

grated rind and juice of ½ lemon

25g (1oz) butter

lamb stock made from boiling some lamb bones with root vegetables and herbs

salt and freshly ground black pepper

8 – 12 noisettes of lamb, neatly tied, with a thin surround of fat

Serves 4

Sewin, Salmon and other Freshwater Fish

Salmon Bread and Butter Pudding

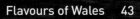

Salmon, Sewin other Freshwa...

The swiftly flowing rivers and streams of Wales have been a ready source of food for centuries. Salmon have always been caught in great number, but it is sewin or sea trout that is held in particular affection by the Welsh.

and er fish

Sewin is a member of the brown trout family. It is similar to salmon, but is distinguishable by the shape of its mouth and the number of scales behind the dorsal fin. Sewin also has a paler pink flesh and more delicate flavour.

Today, the rivers of Wales suffer from dwindling stocks but in years gone by fishing was a way of life and a welcome addition to rural incomes. Some of the fishing methods employed were and remain similar to those used in prehistoric times. Although fish traps have disappeared, men still fish with the aid of nets, and the coracles – still used for sewin and salmon fishing on the Tywi, Teifi and Taf in west Wales – are similar to the skin-covered boats described by Caesar and Pliny. Before the Second World War, coracles were in use on the Dee, Severn and Cleddau and, at the turn of the last century, coracle fishermen were also to

be seen on the rivers Usk, Wye and Conwy. In his account of his travels in south Wales, Benjamin Heath Malkin (1769 – 1842) maintained that the Teifi was '... esteemed the most excellent [salmon river] in Wales. There is scarcely a cottage in the neighbourhood of the Tivy, or the others rivers in these parts abounding with fish, without its coracle hanging by the door.'

One of the oldest forms of fishing involves the use of a seine net, and two or three skilled men are required to loop a net across a river and draw it in full of fish. With particular reference to salmon fishing, George Owen, writing in 1603, said: 'There is also great store of this fish, as also of sewin, mullet and botcher (being all near of kin to the salmon) taken in the said river [Teifi] near St. Dogmael's in a saine net, drawn after every tide...' Today, only one netsman fishes with the aid of a seine net in the Teifi

Estuary, near St. Dogmael's. And putchers or fish-catching baskets made from willow, have all but disappeared from the Severn too.

Today's catches bear no comparison to those of the past for according to J. Geraint Jenkins, author of *Life and Tradition in Rural Wales*, 10,935 salmon and 650 sewin were taken on the Dee in 1882, while on the Severn in the same year the catch amounted to 15,550 salmon. During the summer of 1883 as much as half a ton of salmon were caught in the lower reaches of the Teifi and sent to London. Indeed, so much salmon was available, it made a free meal for many who lived by a river, and labourers and maids working near the Teifi begged not to be given any more by their masters! In some work contracts, 'Salmon served no more than twice a week' was a common clause.

Fillet of Sewin

cooked in paper and served with Lady Llanover's Granville Sauce

Ingredients

Four 275g (6oz) fillets of sewin

1 leek, finely chopped

salt and pepper

1 Place a sewin fillet or portion in the centre of a circle of greaseproof paper.

2 Tuck some leeks under the fish, and scatter a few on top.

3 Season well.

4 Wrap the paper over the fish in order to seal it, and then bake in a medium oven for about 8 – 10 minutes.

Lady Llanover's Granville Sauce

1 small anchovy, pounded in a mortar

1 shallot, finely chopped

2 tablespoons dry sherry

half a tablespoon best vinegar

6 whole peppercorns

a little nutmeg

a very little mace

1 Simmer the combined ingredients very gently, stirring well all the time, until the shallot is soft.

2 Place half an ounce of butter in another saucepan, with as much flour as will make it into a stiff paste.

3 Add the other ingredients which have been simmering and stir well, till scalding hot, for about 2 minutes.

4 Add 6 tablespoons of cream, stir well and strain.

5 Serve the sewin either in or out of the paper, with a garnish of leek and a little of the sauce.

6 A potato and fennel pie makes the perfect accompaniment.

Potato and Fennel Pie

4 large potatoes, scrubbed but not peeled

1 bulb of fennel, scrubbed

2 cloves garlic, crushed

300ml (½ pint) cream

300ml (½ pint) milk

salt and pepper

Serves 4

1 Slice the potatoes and fennel thinly.

2 Butter a large baking dish and arrange the potato slices and the fennel with garlic and seasoning in alternate layers.

3 Pour over the cream and milk, and bake the pie at a moderate heat (375°F [190°C], Gas 5) for 45 – 60 minutes.

Whole Poached Sewin

with Sorrel Mayonnaise

1 Poach the sewin in gently simmering salt water for 4 – 6 minutes per pound.

2 Remove the pan from the stove and leave for ½ hour before lifting the fish from the water.

3 Alternatively, you can parcel the salmon in buttered tinfoil with half a glass of white wine, salt, peppercorns and several slices of lemon, and bake in a moderate oven (350°F [180°C] Gas 4) for ¾ hour.

4 Do not unwrap for 10 minutes or so after removing from the oven.

5 Skin the fish, remove the head and tail and keep to one side.

6 Then carefully lift all four fillets off the bone and wrap each individually in foil until required.

7 Mix all the herbs into the mayonnaise; taste for seasoning.

To serve

1 On a large oval serving dish, reassemble the two underside fillets of salmon and spread a layer of mayonnaise over the top.

2 Place the upper fillets on top and reposition the head and tail.

3 Garnish with thinly sliced cucumber around the head and down the length of the fish.

4 Add lemon slices and bunches of watercress.

5 Serve the remaining mayonnaise separately.

Ingredients

1.8kg – 2.7kg (4 – 6lb) sewin or salmon, whole fish with head and tail

watercress, lemon wedges and cucumber to garnish

300ml (½ pint) home-made mayonnaise or 1 jar best mayonnaise

1 good handful fresh sorrel, chopped

1 good tablespoon fresh dill, chopped

1 good tablespoon chives, chopped

Serves 6 – 8

Garnish with thinly sliced cucumber around the head and down the length of the fish.

Smoked Sewin
and Salmon Terrine

A superb recipe by Sandra Bates when she was at The Crown at Whitebrook on the River Wye

Ingredients

1.5kg (3lbs) fresh salmon fillet

275g (10oz) smoked sewin (or sea trout), thinly sliced

75g (3oz) cucumber, peeled, seeded and diced

75g (3oz) carrots, peeled, diced and blanched for 3 minutes

1 lemon – zest peeled and diced, blanched for 3 minutes

12 quail's eggs, hard boiled and peeled

1 tablespoon mixed parsley, dill and chives, finely chopped

225g (8oz) unsalted butler

50ml (2fl oz) double cream

Fish cooking liquor

600ml (1 pint) fish stock

1 glass white wine

1 small chopped onion

Serves 12

1 Line a terrine dish with cling film and arrange a layer of thinly-sliced smoked sewin across the bottom and up the sides.

2 Set aside some to fold on top of the filling. Reserve any extra pieces of smoked sewin for the filling.

3 Poach the salmon in the cooking liquor for approximately 10 minutes and leave to cool.

4 Reduce the liquor to a thick and syrupy consistency, then add the juice of half the lemon and the double cream.

5 Add the butter bit by bit, season the sauce, strain and leave to cool.

6 Add the flaked salmon to the cool cream mixture, together with the cucumber, carrots, lemon zest, herbs and remaining smoked sewin.

7 Toss carefully together.

8 Place half of the mixture into the terrine.

9 Arrange the quail eggs to make a layer across the middle of the terrine, and fill with the rest of the salmon mixture.

10 Cover with overlapping smoked sewin slices and place the terrine in the fridge for 12 hours.

11 Serve with mixed, dressed salad leaves and fresh wholemeal toast.

Salmon Bread and Butter Pudding

1 Arrange half the bread in the bottom of a baking dish. Pour over the wine.

2 Scatter over the salmon and arrange the remaining bread on top.

3 Whisk the eggs, seasoning, herbs, milk and cream together and pour over the pudding.

4 Bake at 375°F [190°C] Gas 5 for 20 – 30 minutes.

Ingredients

6 slices thinly-sliced bread, spread with garlic butter

1 small glass dry white wine

450g (1lb) fresh fillet of salmon, sliced thinly

6 eggs

salt and pepper

dill and chives

150ml (¼ pint) milk

150ml (¼ pint) single cream

Serves 5 – 6

The boats which they employ in fishing or in crossing the rivers are made of twigs, not oblong nor pointed, but almost round, or rather triangular, covered both within and without with raw hides. When a salmon thrown into one of these boats strikes it hard with his tail, he often oversets it, and endangers both the vessel and its navigator. The fishermen, according to the custom of the country, in going to and from the rivers, carry these boats on their shoulders; on which occasion that famous dealer in fables, Bleddercus, who lived a little before our time, thus mysteriously said: 'There is amongst us a people who, when they are out in search of prey, carry their horses on their back to the place of plunder; in order to catch their prey, they leap upon their horses, and when it is taken, carry their horses home again upon their shoulders.'

Geraldus Cambrensis (c. 1146 –1223).

Once upon a time, during a great famine in north Wales, Saint Brigid came to the rescue of the people by casting into the river a bundle of reeds (*brwyn* in Welsh) which were subsequently transformed into *brwyniaid*. It is said that these rare fish only appear after the snow on the mountain peaks has disappeared. Welsh *brwyniaid* are thought to be sparling or smelts.

In Welsh, an Arctic Char is called a *torgoch*, which means 'red belly'. Char are the least known members of the salmon family, confined to deep, inland lakes. Looking rather like trout – about 25 – 30cm (10 –12 inches) long, with a dark greenish-brown back fading into silver, and a deep red belly – they have pinkish flesh, more delicate than salmon.

Llyn Padarn in north Wales is famous for its stock of *torgoch* but they are no easy fish to catch because they live at great depth. The fisherman in his boat must weigh his line heavily and depend on oars, rather than an engine, because speed causes the line to rise, and an engine would disturb the quiet lake waters. In late summer, the fish surface and head for the river to spawn. At this time, there is more chance of catching a *torgoch* with the aid of a spinner.

Brwyniaid and Arctic Char

Brown Trout

Trout has always been a favourite in Wales. In his famous novel, *How Green Was My Valley*, Richard Llewellyn describes how the catching of brown trout brought great joy to one particular miner:

My father taught me to tickle trout up on the flat rock down by Mrs Tom Jenkins …

First you would have to roll back your sleeve, sometimes up to your muscle, and put your arm right in the water, holding your hand open and steady … Then the old fish would come along very soft and quiet … Of course, you would not move a fraction, even your eyes … because a good and sensible trout will swim back out of reach and stay there to laugh at you … Then it would be your turn. Quietly, you would bend your fingers to smooth him under his stomach and tickle his ribs. Sometimes he would flash away and you would lose him, but oftener he would stay on. Then you would work your fingers along him until your little finger was inside his gill. That was enough. Give him a jerk and pull out your arm, and there he would be, flapping on the rock. And there is good fresh trout for supper. My mother used to put them on a hot stone over the fire, wrapped in breadcrumbs, butter, parsley and lemon rind, all bound about with the fresh green leaves of leeks. If there is better food in heaven, I am in a hurry to be there, if I will not be thought wicked for saying so.

Richard Llewellyn, *How Green Was My Valley* (1939).

Trout Wrapped in Bacon

Ingredients

4 good sized trout

1 tablespoon chopped chives

4 slices lemon

salt and freshly ground black pepper

8 rashers smoked streaky bacon

Horseradish Sauce

Greek yogurt mixed with a little freshly grated horseradish and chopped parsley.

Serves 4

1 Pre-heat the oven to 400°F [200°C], Gas 6.

2 Clean, gut and if possible, bone the trout.

3 (The best way to do this is to open up the trout, spread it tummy down on a board and press hard along the back – this loosens the bones from the flesh. Then, starting at the head end, ease away the backbone with the tip of a knife, removing at the same time as many of the small bones as possible.)

4 Place some chopped chives and a slice of lemon in the belly of each fish, and season with salt and pepper.

5 Wrap each fish in two rashers of bacon and lay them side by side in a baking dish.

6 Bake for 15 – 20 minutes until the bacon is crisp on top and the trout flesh is cooked and flaky.

7 Serve with horseradish sauce.

Place some chopped chives and a slice of lemon in the belly of each fish, and season with salt and pepper.

Potted Trout

1. In a small earthenware pot, or terrine, arrange half the trout fillets in one layer.

2. Scatter over the dill, mace and seasoning.

3. Arrange the remaining trout fillets on top.

4. In a small pan, gently heat the butter until it melts, but does not boil.

5. Pour carefully over the trout fillets so that they are completely covered with butter. (Leave the creamy white sediment from the butter in the bottom of the saucepan.)

6. Cover with foil or a lid and bake the trout in a moderate oven (350°F [180°C] Gas 4) for 20 minutes.

7. Remove from the oven and leave to cool.

8. Chill in the fridge for at least 4 hours for the butter to harden.

9. To make the Melba toast, toast sliced bread on both sides and, while still warm, slit sideways with a sharp knife to make two thin slices.

10. Cut in half, diagonally, then toast the uncooked sides of bread until crisp.

Ingredients

450g (1lb) trout fillets, skinned with all bones removed

225g (8oz) slightly salted, creamy butter

1 tablespoon chopped dill

1 teaspoon ground mace

salt and freshly ground black pepper

fresh warm toast or Melba toast to serve

Leeks

Anglesey Eggs

5

Leeks

Leeks were grown by the Sumerians as long ago as 2,500 BC, but it was their use in Roman kitchens that might well have led to the introduction of leeks, the most Welsh of vegetables, to Wales.

The leek was prized by the Welsh, so much so that they adopted this humble vegetable as an emblem in their battles against the Saxons. Leeks were sported as a cap badge by Welshmen at the battle of Heathfield in 633 AD, and it is reputed that David, the patron saint of Wales, also led troops wearing leeks in their hats. However, a more plausible tale about David, the pilgrim and peacemaker, is that he fed on leeks gathered in the fields. According to tradition, the leek also led Harry of Monmouth, later Henry V, to victory at Agincourt: 'Welshmen did good service,' said Shakespeare, '... wearing leeks in their Monmouth caps [woollen headgear worn by medieval soldiers].'

Henry VII also put the leek to good use at the battle of Crécy, where it was adopted as a secret code amongst his followers to signify their allegiance to the King. As grandson of Katherine of Valois, Henry used the green and white of Valois in his coat of arms, and if his followers met each other in a field, they simply pulled up a blade of grass, a wild hyacinth, a daffodil, or anything that possessed a green stem and white root.

Although the leek did lose its place to the daffodil as the national emblem at the installation of Edward as Prince of Wales, at Caernarfon in July 1911, it can still lay claim to being the national vegetable of Wales, which is sported by many in preference to the daffodil on 1 March, St David's Day.

Leeks are eaten raw by soldiers serving in Welsh regiments, and as a one time army wife, I remember well the odious breath of my beloved on returning from his regimental St David's Day celebrations.

In rural Wales, however, leeks have only recently been accepted as a vegetable in their own right, rather than a flavour for the stew pot or a green garnish in *cawl*. Lady Llanover (Augusta Waddington Hall, 1802 – 96) in her book, *The First Principles of Good Cookery*, published in 1867, refers to leeks many times but always as an ingredient added in order to impart flavour to a stew. She also credits the leek with being a wonderful herb, possessing nutritional as well as medicinal qualities.

To prepare leeks, always wash well and if using the whole stem, slit down the length and run cold water through from top to bottom. Leeks steam well and cook very satisfactorily in the microwave in a minimum of water. To retain the bright green colour of cooked leeks, rinse under cold water as soon as they are cooked.

Anglesey Eggs

Ingredients

450g (1lb) potatoes, peeled

3 leeks, washed and chopped

50g (2oz) butter

50g (2oz) flour

600ml (1 pint) milk

75g (3oz) Cheddar cheese, grated

salt and freshly ground black pepper

4 eggs, hard boiled and shelled

Serves 4

1 Boil the potatoes in salted water until soft. Cook the leeks in salted water for 10 minutes, or add to the potatoes for the last 10 minutes of their cooking time.

2 Drain well, then combine, season and mash together.

3 Make a cheese sauce by melting the butter in a saucepan, stir in the flour and cook for a minute.

4 Gradually stir in the milk and bring to the boil to thicken. Season well and add half the cheese.

5 Take four individual dishes or one family dish and, with the aid of a fork, arrange the leek and potato mixture around the sides.

6 Slice the eggs in half and put an egg into each individual dish or all the eggs into the larger dish.

7 Cover with the cheese sauce and sprinkle over the remaining cheese.

8 Brown quickly under a hot grill or heat through in a very hot oven (450°F [230°C], Gas 8) for 10 minutes.

Make a cheese sauce by melting the butter in a saucepan, stir in the flour and cook for a minute.

Leek and Goat's Cheese Parcels

1 Discard the tough outer leaves of the leeks and wash them under cold running water.

2 Keep them whole and plunge into a large saucepan of boiling water.

3 Boil for 8 minutes, drain and run under the cold tap. This will cool them quickly and also maintain the bright green colour.

4 Peel the layers off the leeks, tearing as little as possible.

5 Set the best eight layers aside and finely chop the remainder.

6 Mix the chopped leeks, goat's cheese, walnuts and raisins, and divide the mixture into four portions.

7 Wrap each portion in two of the layers of leek, making a parcel shape.

8 Arrange the leek parcels on a serving dish.

9 Place all the ingredients for the dressing into a jam jar and shake well to blend.

10 Spoon some dressing over each parcel.

Ingredients

2 medium-sized leeks

100g (4oz) fresh goat's cheese

50g (2oz) walnuts, chopped

25g (1oz) raisins, soaked in sherry for 30 minutes

For the dressing

3 tablespoons walnut oil

1 tablespoon white wine vinegar

1 teaspoon runny honey

salt and freshly ground black pepper

Serves 4

Casserole of Leeks

with Cream and Parsley

Ingredients

1.2kg (2lbs) leeks, slim and young, if possible

2 tablespoons chopped parsley

good pinch of grated nutmeg

salt and black pepper

25g (1oz) butter

150ml (¼ pint) double cream

125g (5oz) strong Welsh Cheddar

Serves 4 – 6

1 Preheat the oven to 350°F [180°C], Gas 4.

2 Slice the leeks into 1cm (½ inch) lengths and wash well. Place them in a large ovenproof dish.

3 Sprinkle the parsley over the leeks, add nutmeg and seasoning, and dot with butter.

4 Cover the dish and place in the oven to cook for 15 minutes.

5 Pour the cream over the leeks and sprinkle with grated cheese.

6 Brown under a hot grill and serve at once as a side dish to a roast, or on its own, with chunks of fresh granary bread.

Sprinkle the parsley over the leeks, add nutmeg and seasoning, and dot with butter.

Leek, Bacon and Cheese Soufflé

1. Heat the oven to 425ºF [215°C], Gas 7.

2. Dry-fry the bacon in a heavy-based casserole dish until crisp.

3. Add the butter, leeks and mushrooms and cook until soft.

4. Stir in the flour and allow to cook a little before adding the milk slowly, stirring well.

5. Add the cheese, grated or in small chunks.

6. After the cheese has melted, leave the mixture to cool slightly.

7. Stir the egg yolks and seasoning into the mixture.

8. Whisk the eggs whites until stiff and fold these into the soufflé, using a large metal spoon, stirring until all sign of the egg whites has gone.

9. Cook the soufflé in the pre-heated oven for 20 – 25 minutes until it rises and the top is golden brown in colour.

10. Serve at once with chunks of fresh bread and a dry white wine.

Ingredients

8 rashers of streaky bacon, rinded and chopped

50g (2oz) butter

2 medium-sized leeks, washed and finely sliced

100g (4oz) mushrooms, sliced

2 heaped tablespoons plain flour

425ml (¾ pint) milk

100g (4oz) Cheddar cheese

6 eggs, separated

salt and freshly ground black pepper

Serves 3 – 4

Leek Pesto with Baked Salmon

Ingredients

2 medium leeks

100g (4oz) pine nuts

1 clove garlic

4 tablespoons olive oil

salt and pepper

4 – 6 portions of fillet of salmon

Serves 4 – 6

1 Wash and chop the leeks roughly.

2 In a food processor or liquidiser, blend the leeks, nuts, garlic, olive oil and seasoning. Continue blending until you have a smooth sauce.

3 Place each portion of salmon on a 25cm (10 inch) square piece of greaseproof paper or foil.

4 Add a good teaspoonful of the leek pesto and fold the sides of the paper over to make a panel.

5 Squeeze the edges together to seal the parcel.

6 Bake the salmon parcels for 8 – 10 minutes in a hot oven (425°F [220°C] Gas 7).

7 Serve the salmon and pesto with steamed leek puddings.

Steamed Leek Puddings

1 Split the leeks lengthways and wash well.

2 Plunge them into a shallow pan of boiling water and simmer for a few minutes until soft.

3 Rinse under a cold tap to retain the bright green colour.

4 Using a combination of light and dark green leaves, line four dariole moulds or ramekins.

5 Set aside the remaining leeks. Process or blend the bread to make crumbs.

6 Add the leeks, eggs and double cream and blend until you have a smooth, dropping consistency.

7 Add extra breadcrumbs if the mixture is too runny, or extra milk to soften.

8 Season with paprika, ginger and parsley and place the mixture into the lined moulds. Fold over excess leek leaf to make secure parcels and steam the moulds or cook in a *bain-marie* for approximately 20 minutes, until firm to touch.

Ingredients

4 good sized leeks

2 slices wholemeal bread

2 eggs

120ml (4fl oz) double cream

salt and pepper

pinch of paprika

pinch of grated fresh ginger

1 tablespoon chopped parsley

Season with paprika, ginger and parsley and place the mixture into the lined moulds.

Welsh Lamb

Welsh Spring Lamb with Leeks and Mead

6

Welsh La

Due to modern farming methods, Welsh lamb today is lean, tender and tasty. But what of its origins?

Little is known of the early development of Welsh Mountain Sheep, and detailed descriptions of the breed do not appear until the late 18th century.

However, these sheep, which have roamed the hills for centuries, are known for their hardiness and suitability to withstand the severe winter climate and poor mountain pastures of Snowdonia, Cader Idris, Plynlimon and the Brecon Beacons. A Welsh Mountain Sheep Society was established in 1905 with the aim of fostering and improving the breed. Today's ewes are good mothers and excellent milkers, and will fatten their lambs on poor pastures, if given the freedom to run.

Welsh lamb is considered by many to be the best in the world. This may be due to the fact that over a hundred years ago Welsh lamb and mutton was sent by hamper to London where it was received by the wealthy as a cachet of good taste. Indeed, it was in the early 19th century that Edward Hamer's family firm was established by Solomon Hamer. Solomon began by slaughtering some sheep on his small-holding in Trefeglwys and selling them in Llanidloes Market on a Saturday. So successful was the venture that Solomon opened a small shop in China Street, Llanidloes.

His eldest son, Edward, was sent to London to learn the meat trade. Here, he realised that there was a demand for quality meat and returned home with the idea of selling Hamer lamb in London. After a difficult start, the business flourished and Edward built new, prestigious premises in Longbridge Street, Llanidloes. A finer example of a Victorian butcher's shop would be hard to find, and at the back of the original premises there stood a slaughterhouse and cutting rooms. From here Edward packaged his lamb and sent it to London in his own railway carriages on the 7:49 p.m. train from Llanidloes arriving at Euston at 3:50 a.m.

The hallmark of success came in 1889 when the Warrant of Appointment as Purveyors to Queen Victoria was received, and it was a proud moment for the townspeople of Llanidloes when the Royal Coat of Arms arrived and was erected above the shop. Later, they were appointed purveyors to King Edward VII and King George V. In time, Hamers also supplied a great number of Officers' Messes and eventually received seven Royal warrants for the quality of their Welsh mutton, the produce of the Plynlimon area.

Tis the Plynlimon herbage
That flavours the meat
And makes it nutritious
Delicious and sweet.

According to one observer, 'Welsh Mountain Sheep, as found on Plynlimon are a distinct breed, and termed the Plynlimon Welsh. They are small, extremely active, and delight in lofty situations during the summer months. In the early autumn they are brought down from the mountains to the richer pastures of the Severn valley, to be fattened for our English trade. Compact, neat, and small of bone, they command favour wherever introduced.'

Alas, rationing during the Second World War put an end to the pre-war trade, but the name Hamer is still strongly linked with Welsh lamb and the family has fine shops in Llanidloes, Rhayader and Machynlleth. Since taking over the family firm twenty-five years ago, Edward Hamer junior has added a spanking new abattoir, built in 1992, the first Grade 1 HHC-approved abattoir in Britain. Furthermore, he sells his lamb in Greece, southern Italy, Spain and most other European countries. Not content with Hamers the retail butchers, Hamers the wholesale butchers, Hamers the fast-food venue on the show ground, Hamers the abattoir and Hamers the carcass salesman in the EEC, Edward Hamer wants to be known as *Hamers the lamb*, worldwide!

Spiced Lamb

Hams made from Welsh mutton were often cured at home, cleaned and salted with a mixture of salt, brown sugar and spices, and then hung up the chimney to be smoked. Another way of presenting lamb was to spice it. This recipe was given to me by Ann Owston.

Ingredients

1 breast of lamb

2 teaspoons salt

1 teaspoon black pepper

a pinch of ground allspice and cloves

Dry marinade

40g (1½oz) rock sea salt

6g (¼oz) saltpetre (optional)

12g (½oz) soft brown sugar

1 Remove the bones from the breast of lamb, cut away excess fat and sprinkle over the salt, black pepper, ground allspice and cloves.

2 Roll up the lamb and tie or secure with cocktail sticks.

3 Rub over the dry marinade mixture of rock salt, saltpetre and soft brown sugar.

4 Turn the lamb and leave in the fridge for up to a week, recoating with the marinade mixture daily.

5 Rinse the lamb well under a cold tap, place in a pan and cover with cold water. Simmer for at least 1 hour, until soft when pierced.

6 Leave the lamb to cool in the cooking liquid, then drain and transfer to the fridge, and cover with a weight for at least 12 hours.

7 Serve cold, thinly sliced with sweet, fruity chutney.

Leave in the fridge for up to a week, recoating with the marinade mixture daily.

Roast Leg of Welsh Lamb

with Ginger, Honey, Cider and Rosemary

1 Peel the ginger and cut the slivers. Using a sharp knife, make small cuts in the leg of lamb and insert the ginger.

2 Mix the butter, honey and rosemary together and spread over the lamb. Place in a roasting dish, pour in half of the cider, and cover loosely with foil.

3 Roast in a moderately hot oven (375°F [190°C] Gas 5), allowing 25 minutes per pound.

4 When three-quarters cooked, remove the foil and continue cooking, basting frequently with the juices from the roasting tin, and adding more cider, if necessary.

5 Remove the joint from the oven, lift out of the pan and keep warm.

6 Strain the juices from the pan, removing the excess fat, and pour in the rest of the cider to 'deglaze' the pan.

7 Boil this up well, return the non-fatty juices and thicken with a little arrowroot if you wish.

8 A well-seasoned, mixed mash of carrot, parsnip, turnip and potatoes tastes perfect with this roast leg of lamb.

Ingredients

1 leg of lamb weighing about 1.5kg (3lb 5oz)

2.5cm (1 inch) piece of fresh root ginger

25g (1oz) butter, melted

2 tablespoons honey

1 tablespoon fresh rosemary, finely chopped

250ml (9fl oz) dry cider

salt and freshly ground black pepper

Serves 6

The leg of mutton of Wales beats the leg of mutton of any other country, and I had never tasted a Welsh leg of mutton before. Certainly I shall never forget the first Welsh leg of mutton which I tasted, rich but delicate, replete with juices derived from the aromatic herbs of the noble Berwyn, cooked to a turn and weighing just four pounds.

George Borrow, *Wild Wales* (1862).

Drover's Pie

Anne Newcombe gave me this recipe. She lives at Feeding Ground Cottage, near Kerry, in the Camlad valley, a route once followed by drovers. In the past, when drovers walked their livestock from the uplands of Wales to the English lowlands and towns, they followed established routes. Welcome resting places for both man and beast were sometimes marked by the planting of three Scotch pine trees. Nearby, a friendly farmer would provide food for all.

Ingredients

350g (12oz) raw, minced lamb

175g (6oz) onion, chopped

100g (4oz) mushrooms, chopped

1 small sprig fresh mint, chopped (or 1 teaspoon dried mint)

1 garlic clove, chopped or pressed

1 tablespoon oil

12 nasturtium seeds, halved (or capers) (optional)

150ml (5fl oz) stock (thicken with 1 tablespoon cornflour)

salt and pepper to taste

225g (8oz) shortcrust pastry

450g (1lb) cooked potatoes mashed with 1 tablespoon milk and 1 tablespoon butter

Serves 2 – 3 or one hungry drover!

1 Pre-heat the oven to 400ºF (200ºC), Gas 6.

2 Grease and line a one-pint, ovenproof pie dish with pastry.

3 Heat the oil in a heavy pan and fry the onions, garlic and mushrooms for 4 – 5 minutes.

4 Add the lamb and fry, stirring occasionally until the meat is browned.

5 Stir in the nasturtiums, mint, salt, pepper and stock.

6 Bring to the simmer and then remove from the heat, and cool.

7 Cook and mash the potatoes.

8 Place the mince mixture into the pastry shell, spread mashed potato over the filling, and smooth with a round-bladed knife.

9 Finally, pattern the surface with a fork.

10 Place the pie dish on a baking tray and cook in a hot oven for 30 minutes.

11 Serve with fresh green vegetables.

Real Welsh mutton was admitted by all epicures, and by medical men, to be the very finest for flavour, and the lightest of digestion of all the breeds of sheep.

Lady Llanover

Welsh Spring Lamb

with Leeks and Mead

1 Pre-heat the oven to 450°F [230°C], Gas 8.

2 Trim the lamb so as to leave a minimum of fat and ensure the bones are scraped clean away from the nut of meat.

3 Interlock the bones and tuck them under the meat to prevent them burning.

4 Oven roast the lamb in hot oil in a roasting tin for about 15 minutes, or a little longer if you prefer your meat well done.

5 Wash and shred the leek into the finest matchsticks.

6 Heat the butter in a pan and fry the leeks gently until soft.

7 Sprinkle over the thyme and season well.

8 Once the lamb is cooked, dish up the racks and leave to rest for five minutes.

9 For the gravy, pour the fat from the roasting pan, then add the mead and boil up well.

10 Stir in the redcurrant jelly and allow the sauce to thicken slightly.

11 To serve, cut down between the lamb chops and serve three to a plate with a spoonful of the leeks as an accompaniment.

12 Pour the gravy round each plate.

Ingredients

2 best ends (or racks) of Welsh spring lamb (each strip with 6 chops)

1 glass dry mead or cider

1 tablespoon redcurrant jelly

1 leek

2 teaspoons fresh thyme, chopped

seasoning

Serves 6

Serve three to a plate with a spoonful of leeks as an accompaniment.

Crown Roast of Welsh Lamb with Leek and Laverbread Stuffing, and Laverbread Sauce

A crown roast is shaped from two racks of lamb tied together, with the excess skin trimmed away to expose the bones. To ensure that it cooks evenly, it is best to cook the meat and stuffing separately and to add the stuffing after cooking.

To ensure that it cooks evenly, it is best to cook the meat and stuffing separately.

① Slit the lamb and stuff the garlic slivers into the meat.

② Roast the crown at 400ºF [200ºC], Gas 6 for 30 – 45 minutes, depending on how rare you like your lamb.

Ingredients

2 trimmed loins of lamb, 750y – 1kg (1½ – 2lb) each

2 cloves garlic, cut into slivers

---

① Dry-fry the bacon until the fat runs.

② Add the leeks and butter, and fry until soft.

③ Stir in the laverbread, orange rind and juice, and enough fresh breadcrumbs to form a firm stuffing.

④ Season to taste.

⑤ Add the beaten egg to bind.

⑥ Bake for 30 minutes underneath the lamb.

⑦ Spoon into the crown roast for the last 10 minutes.

Leek and Laverbread Stuffing

2 rashers streaky bacon, diced

1 good sized leek, washed and shredded

50g (2oz) Welsh butter

50g (2oz) laverbread

½ orange, grated rind and squeezed juice

breadcrumbs

1 egg, beaten

---

① Deglaze the roasting tin with the dry white wine.

② Pour in the laverbread, the citrus peel and juices and bring the sauce to the boil.

③ Simmer until the consistency is syrupy, and add the butter, piece by piece.

Laverbread Sauce

50g (2oz) freshly pulped laverbread

1 glass dry white wine

juice and finely grated rind of ½ orange

juice of ½ lemon

25g (1oz) butter

seasoning

Welsh Beef

Beef, Beer and Rosemary Cobbler

Welsh Be

Welsh Blacks, referred to in early Welsh literature, have been the native cattle of Wales since pre Roman times.

Originally of different character in different parts of Wales, two distinct strains had developed by the late 19th century – the smaller compact north Wales cattle and the bigger, rangier south Wales or Castlemartin type. Lady Llanover wrote with affection about the black cattle of Carmarthen and Pembroke in her book *The First Principles of Good Cookery* (1867): 'The Pembroke, or Castle-Martin breed, is admirable for beef, and they are excellent milkers.' And with reference to the Welsh Blacks of north Wales she has this to say:

In North Wales the Mona breed (Isle of Anglesea) is the best, and is equal, if not superior, by various combined excellences, to the larger breeds in Wales, and, like other Welsh cattle, are very hardy. It is remarkable for its small size, with great symmetry, mild temper, large supply of rich milk, and ability to feed and do well on short pasture, and also to fatten with the greatest ease, and for beef it cannot be surpassed.

Lady Llanover, *The First Principles of Good Cookery* (1867).

The Welsh Black Cattle Society, established in 1873, sought to improve the native strains in Wales. Cross-breeding resulted in the development of the modern Welsh Black, a much improved animal and an ideal, hardy, suckler animal, producing a first-class butcher's beast.

Welsh Blacks, which thrive in the Welsh climate and on the hills of Wales, have a sturdy frame and placid temperament. From a farmer's point of view, they are a pleasure to breed for not only are they hardy, but the females are also noted for easy calving and their mothering ability. Furthermore, their remarkable digestive system makes them the easiest and cheapest cattle to feed. Neither cold nor rain seems to bother them, and during the winter they develop a superb thick coat, which is usually shed in spring.

However, up until the last decade the Welsh Black breed had suffered from being too small for the butcher and their fatty meat found no favour with customers. As a consequence, they were replaced on many Welsh farms by the large, lean continental breeds. Now, with good breeding and a diet of natural herbage, these excellent beef cattle are making a strong comeback. Today, as a response to the customer's insistence on flavour and marbling in beef, prices are rising in the market place, and since farmers are looking to home-grown stock, you can now see many of these fine black cattle grazing Welsh pastures.

Sirloin of Welsh Black Beef

with Leek Batter Puddings and Horseradish Cream

Ingredients

1.4kg – 1.8kg (3 – 4lbs) sirloin of Welsh Black beef, boned and rolled.

1 Roast the meat in a hot oven (450°F [230°C] Gas 8) and reduce the heat after 15 minutes to 400°F [200°C], Gas 6.

2 When cooking, allow 15 minutes per pound, and an extra 15 minutes. (A 1.4kg [3lb] joint will therefore take an hour to cook.)

3 Once cooked, allow the beef to rest in a warm place for a further 15 minutes, for the juices to settle. This also makes the meat firmer to carve.

4 About 20 minutes before you are ready to dish up, pop the batter puddings into the top of the oven.

Leek Batter Puddings

1 leek, finely chopped

300ml (½ pint) milk

100g (4oz) plain flour

1 egg

salt and pepper

1 Cook the leek in a minimum of water in a saucepan, or in the microwave, until barely soft. Leave to cool.

2 Make a batter with the milk, flour, egg and seasoning.

3 Add the leek. Pour the batter into a hot, 12-bun tray which has a little oil in the bottom of each compartment.

4 Bake for 20 minutes until risen and golden brown.

Horseradish Cream

4 tablespoons *crème fraîche*, or double cream, softly whipped

1 teaspoon freshly grated horseradish, or creamed horseradish from a bottle

a pinch of mustard, salt and pepper

Serves 6 – 8

1 Mix the sauce ingredients together.

2 To serve, arrange the leek batter puddings around the meat.

3 The horseradish cream should be served separately.

Beef, Beer and Rosemary Cobbler

1. Pre-heat the oven to 300°F [150°C], Gas 2.

2. Cut the fat and sinew off the beef and kidneys and dice into 2.5cm (1 inch) chunks, and toss in the seasoned flour.

3. Heat the dripping or oil in a heavy-based casserole dish and fry the meat, a little at a time so that it browns on all sides.

4. Remove from the pan and fry the onions, leeks and carrots gently until they colour.

5. Replace the meat and add the liquid, herbs and tomato puree. Cover and cook gently for 2 hours.

Ingredients

750g (1½lb) beef (stewing or shin)

225g (8oz) lamb's kidneys

seasoned plain flour

50g (2oz) dripping or 2 tablespoons cooking oil

2 onions, diced

2 leeks, washed and sliced

2 carrots, scrubbed and sliced

300ml (½ pint) beef stock

300ml (½ pint) brown ale

1 teaspoon fresh rosemary, finely chopped

1 tablespoon tomato puree

---

1. Rub the butter into the flour, stir in the salt and herbs.

2. Mix the beaten egg with a little milk and add to the flour to make a soft dough.

3. Roll or pat out the dough on a floured surface.

4. Cut into circles with a small cutter.

5. Remove the casserole dish from the oven and increase the heat to 425°F [220°C], Gas 7.

6. Place the scones, overlapping one another, on top of the meat.

7. Brush with milk, return to the hot oven and bake for 10 – 15 minutes until the crust is golden brown.

For the scone topping

75g (3oz) butter

225g (8oz) self-raising flour

salt

1 teaspoon rosemary, finely chopped

1 egg

milk to mix

Serves 4 – 6

Welsh Pork

Welsh Faggots in Gravy

Welsh Por...

As you tuck into a good Welsh breakfast, consider the past glory of the Welsh pig.

During the 19th century and up to the early 1950s, pigs were a vital part of the rural economy. They provided food in a variety of forms to feed the family from January to December. The pig was tended throughout the year, growing fat on potato trimmings and greens grown in the vegetable plot, and in the autumn it would be turned loose to root out acorns, windfalls, and grain left in the fields after the harvest. In late autumn, however, a travelling butcher would be called upon to slaughter the pig. This was an important social occasion. The fresh offal would, without delay, be made into faggots, and a friend who still remembers the occasion well, recalls how the gall bladder from the poor creature would be blown up and used as a football by the children. All the good cuts were salted and left to cure, before being hung on large hooks in the kitchen ready to feed the family and visitors during the year. Bacon, lean strips interspersed with thick fat, would be fried to feed the farmer at breakfast time, and the last ham was often kept for the harvest supper the following autumn. Fat bacon, so fatty that there is hardly any lean meat to be seen, is still sold in Carmarthen Market. The flavour is superb and many housewives keep some to add a good rich flavour to their cooking.

Boiled Ham and Parsley Sauce

Ingredients

1.8kg – 2.2kg (4 – 5lb) horseshoe of gammon

2 tablespoons dark brown sugar

1 teaspoon Welsh wholegrain mustard

1 tablespoon Worcester sauce

1. Soak the gammon in cold water for 3 – 4 hours, then drain and cover with fresh water in a large saucepan.

2. Bring to the boil and change the water again.

3. Cook the ham at a very gentle simmer for 2 hours.

4. Remove the skin and cut a lattice pattern across the remaining fat.

5. Wrap the ham in foil and bake in the oven for 45 minutes at 350°F [180°C], Gas 4.

6. Combine the sugar, mustard and Worcester sauce and spread the paste over the surface of the ham, and bake uncovered for 15 minutes until the coating bubbles.

7. Serve with parsley sauce.

Parsley Sauce

600ml (1 pint) milk

2 heaped tablespoons plain flour

salt and pepper

a good handful of fresh parsley, stalks and all

50g (2oz) butter

Serves 8

1. Liquidise the milk, flour, seasoning and parsley.

2. In a saucepan, melt the butter and add the milk mixture.

3. Bring the sauce to the boil, stirring continuously until it thickens.

Cook the ham at a very gentle simmer for 2 hours.

Welsh Faggots in Onion Gravy

The word faggot means 'a bundle', originally sticks bound with twine, and the Welsh faggot is exactly that: bits of pork bundled together and wrapped in the lacy web of caul fat. Not only does the caul help to keep the bundle together, but it also serves to moisten it. In France, faggots are called *crepinette*, literally 'lace'. Some Welsh rugby clubs still serve faggots and peas after matches.

1 Soak the caul (if available) in warm water for 20 minutes before using.

2 In a food processor, chop finely the liver, belly of pork, onions and apples.

3 Blend these well with the breadcrumbs, herbs and seasonings, and then bind with the beaten egg.

4 Using wet hands, shape the mixture into round faggots the size of a small egg, wrap each in a square of caul and arrange closely together in a baking tray.

5 (If you prefer to lay the caul over the top of the faggots, the effect is the same and the process much quicker.)

6 If no caul is available, cover the faggots with a layer of well buttered foil and bake in a moderate oven (350°F [180°C], Gas 4) for about 45 minutes.

7 Test by piercing the faggots to see if the juices run clear.

8 Towards the end of the cooking time, turn up the heat a little and allow the faggots to brown on top.

Ingredients

350g (12oz) pig's liver

225g (8oz) belly of pork

2 onions

1 cooking apple

50g (2oz) fresh breadcrumbs

1 teaspoon chopped sage leaves

a good pinch of nutmeg

a good pinch of ground ginger

salt and freshly milled black pepper

1 egg, beaten

pig's or lamb's caul (optional)

Serves 4

Onion Gravy

1 Peel and finely chop an onion.

2 Cook it very gently in 25g (1oz) lard, butter or oil, until soft and transparent.

3 Turn up the heat and cook the onion until it is a rich brown colour.

4 Stir in a tablespoon of plain flour and continue to cook until the flour has turned a golden brown.

5 Now add 300ml (½ pint) of good brown stock and bring to the boil.

6 Season well.

Game and Poultry

Rabbit with Wholegrain Mustard, Leeks and Thyme

Game and

Although the Celts are credited with introducing animal husbandry to Wales, it is hard to imagine a time when the Welsh did not hunt for game to supplement their diet: pigeon, pheasant, snipe, woodcock, hare, rabbit, duck and, of course, venison.

Poultry

Today, venison is mainly farmed in the Brecon area and at Llansoy in the Usk Valley. As for pheasants, driving through the Ceiriog Valley in north-east Wales is slow going at times due to the pheasants strutting along the road. These birds are now reared for shoots. Rabbit catching once played a vital part in the rural economy and many a family survived on the income generated from selling rabbits in local markets. Rabbit stew still goes down well in the country.

Warm Salad of Pigeon Breast

with Walnuts

Ingredients

4 rashers of streaky bacon, diced

100g (4oz) field mushrooms

12 walnuts, shelled

2 pigeon breasts, cut into slivers

1 dessertspoon cider vinegar

2 tablespoons walnut oil

a selection of salad leaves

chopped parsley to garnish

Serves 4 – 6

1 Arrange the clean, dry salad leaves on four individual plates.

2 In a large, heavy-based frying pan, gently dry-fry the bacon until the fat runs.

3 Add the mushrooms and allow them to absorb the bacon fat.

4 Add the walnuts and turn up the heat, stirring all the time. Add half the oil, toss in the slivers of pigeon breast and stir over brisk heat to seal on all sides and cook thoroughly.

5 Scatter the pigeon, bacon, mushrooms and walnuts over the lettuce, and deglaze the pan with the cider vinegar, heating gently and stirring to collect the juices.

6 Take the pan off the heat, add the remaining oil, blend well and pour at once over the salads.

Deglaze the pan with the cider vinegar, heating gently and stirring to collect the juices.

Venison Steak with Coriander and Orange

on a Potato and Leek Rosti

Farmed venison is the leanest of meats with a gentle, gamey flavour. It should be cooked as lean beef but the accompanying flavours should be those traditional to game.

1 Crush the coriander seeds in a pestle and mortar or with the back of a knife blade.

2 Combine them with the wine, orange rind and the oil and pour over the venison steaks.

3 Leave to marinate for at least an hour before cooking.

4 To prepare the rosti, grate the potato and leek and mix together with the seasoning.

5 Divide and shape into four patties and fry over gentle heat.

6 Turn once to cook both sides. Drain the venison from the marinade and pat dry on kitchen paper.

7 Fry briskly to seal both sides, then lower the heat and fry for another 4 minutes until cooked, but pink in the middle.

8 Slice the steaks.

9 Place a rosti on each serving plate, arrange the venison slices on top and keep warm.

10 Add the marinade to the steak-pan juices and stir well.

11 Add the orange juice and redcurrant jelly and boil to reduce by half.

12 Taste for seasoning and pour around the steaks.

Ingredients

4 venison loin steaks, weighing about 175g (6oz) each

1 glass red wine

1 tablespoon coriander seeds

½ orange, grated rind and juice

1 tablespoon redcurrant jelly

1 tablespoon olive oil

salt and freshly ground black pepper

2 large potatoes, peeled

1 small leek, washed

Serves 4

Raised Game Pie

A fine pie which is often served after a day's shooting at the Griffin Inn, Llyswen. The filling must be prepared the day before you make the pie.

Ingredients

For the filling

1 pheasant, plucked and drawn

½ teaspoon thyme

2 bay leaves

1 level dessertspoon salt

24 black peppercorns

1 large carrot, chopped

1 stick celery, chopped

1 large onion, chopped

275g (10oz) assorted cooked meats, diced (i.e. chicken, ham and whatever game is available)

150ml (¼ pint) red wine

1 tablespoon mixed fresh herbs, or 1 teaspoon dried herbs

For the pastry case

120g (4½oz) lard

150ml (¼ pint water)

350g (12oz) plain flour

½ teaspoon salt

1 egg yolk

beaten egg to glaze

Serves 4 – 6

1 Place the pheasant in a large saucepan with the herbs, seasoning and chopped carrots, celery and onion.

2 Add enough cold water to cover and bring to the boil.

3 Simmer for about 90 minutes until tender.

4 Leave to cool in the liquid. Strip the flesh from the pheasant carcass, and reserve the pheasant stock.

5 In a large bowl, combine the chopped pheasant with the other cooked meats.

6 Pour over the red wine and stir in the fresh herbs.

7 Cover and leave overnight in a cool place.

8 Pre-heat the oven to 400°F [200°C], Gas 6.

9 Grease a loose-bottomed 15cm (6 inch) diameter tin and dust with flour.

10 Melt the fat over a gentle heat.

11 Bring the water to the boil, then remove from the heat and tip in the sieved flour and salt. Stir well to combine.

12 Make a well in the mixture and pour in the melted fat and egg yolk.

13 Beat hard to make a dough and knead into a smooth ball. Keep warm.

14 Roll out three-quarters of the pastry into a large circle and line the tin.

15 Spoon the prepared filling into the case.

16 Roll out the remaining pastry to make a lid and seal the edges with cold water.

17 Prepare a design for the lid and make a 5mm (¼ inch) hole in the centre.

18 Glaze with beaten egg.

19 Bake for 15 minutes then turn the oven down to 325°F [160°C], Gas 3 for another 60 – 90 minutes.

20 Re-heat the pheasant stock and boil hard to reduce to about 300ml (½ pint).

21 Pour the warm stock through the hole in the cooked pie, until full. Leave to cool.

22 Serve the raised game pie, cut into slices, with a side salad and relishes.

Breast of Duck
with Damsons or Plums

1 Heat a heavy-based casserole dish and gently dry-fry the duck for about 5 minutes, breast-side down until the fat melts and the skin is golden brown.

2 Add the vinegar, honey, fruit, spice and seasoning.

3 Cover the pan and simmer for 15 – 20 minutes.

4 Remove the duck and slice onto a serving dish.

5 Drain off the excess fat and reduce the juices until syrupy. Serve with the duck.

Ingredients

4 duck breasts

6 – 8 good sized plums

1 – 2 tablespoons balsamic vinegar

1 tablespoon honey

salt and pepper

pinch of cinnamon

Serves 4

Dry-fry the duck breast-side down until the fat melts and the skin is golden brown.

Salt Duck

with Onion Sauce

Ingredients

1.75kg – 2.25kg (4 – 5lb) duck

100g (4oz) sea salt

2 medium onions, chopped

50ml (2fl oz) water

1 level tablespoon plain flour

300ml (10fl oz) milk

Serves 4 – 6

1 Rub the salt well into the flesh of the duck, turning and recoating every day for 3 days.

2 Keep the duck in a cool place throughout the salting process.

3 Thoroughly rinse the salt off the duck and place it into a large pan or casserole.

4 Pour over cold water to cover, bring to the boil and simmer very gently for 1½ hours, turning over half way through.

5 Stew the chopped onion very, very gently in the water for about 15 minutes, until tender. (It may be necessary to press some greaseproof paper down on top of the onions to retain the moisture.)

6 Strain off the liquid and blend it with the flour, using a whisk.

7 Add the milk and then return the mixture to the onions.

8 Bring the onion sauce to the boil.

9 Simmer for a minute or two in order to cook the flour and thicken the sauce.

10 Either liquidise or sieve the sauce, and taste for seasoning.

11 Serve the duck sliced with the sauce. A fruity chutney tastes great with this dish.

For a common-sized duck, a quarter of a pound of salt, to be well rubbed in and re-rubbed, and turned on a dish every day for three days; then wash all the salt off clean, put it into a double (saucepan) with half a pint of water to the pound, and let it simmer steadily for two hours. Salt boiled duck, with which onion sauce, is much better than roast duck …

Onion Sauce … cut up four onions and stew in a double with a little water until tender; then pour off the water and mix half an ounce of flour with it; then add half a pint of milk, and stir well until of a proper consistency, then pass through a wire sieve and return into the double saucepan; stir well, and when quite hot it is ready to pour over.

Lady Llanover, *The First Principles of Good Cookery* (1867).

Rabbit with Wholegrain Mustard, Leeks and Thyme

1 In a large, heavy-based casserole dish, heat the oil and butter and fry the rabbit until golden brown on all sides.

2 Remove the rabbit and toss in the leeks and garlic.

3 Stir until they begin to soften and then add enough flour to absorb the oil.

4 Stir in the mustard, pour over the stock and replace the rabbit.

5 Add the thyme, salt and pepper. Cover the pan and cook very gently for 1½ hours, until tender, stirring occasionally.

6 Add the cream and stir until well blended.

7 Taste for seasoning, and add some fresh lemon juice, if necessary.

Ingredients

750g (1.5lb) jointed rabbit

1 tablespoon sunflower oil

25g (1oz) butter

4 good leeks, washed and sliced

2 cloves garlic, crushed

1 – 2 tablespoons plain flour

2 tablespoons wholegrain mustard

300 – 450ml (½ – ¾ pint) chicken stock

a good sprig of fresh thyme

salt and pepper

150ml (¼ pint) thick cream or *crème fraîche*

fresh lemon juice to taste

Caerphilly Cheese

Merlin Cheesy Potato and Bacon Layer

Caerphilly

There are many farmhouse cheeses made in Wales today but Caerphilly is still the most famous. Quick to ripen, with a salty yet creamy taste, good Caerphilly is hard to beat and the Welsh love it.

There is a delicious cream-coloured cheese named after the town of Caerphilly in South Wales, but, alas, so I am told by grocers, no longer made there. This is a delightful cheese and I would rather eat it in a field with bread and butter than endure the pretentious luncheon of most wayside hotels.

H. V. Morton, *In Search of Wales* (1932).

Cheese

Caerphilly can be sold relatively young, so bringing a quick return to the cheesemaker, a fact not overlooked by many a Welsh farmer. In a dairy-rich region like Wales, cheesemaking has been a vital part of rural life, brined cheese (a cheese soaked in salty water for a few hours to improve the flavour), such as Caerphilly, was part of the settlement between feuding members of a family, according to the Laws of Hywel Dda (Hywel the Good), a Welsh tenth-century prince, whose laws were administered in lawcourts throughout Wales. Caerphilly was a favourite with miners too. Professor Rhys, of the Royal Commission on Land in Wales and Monmouthshire in 1895, has this to say about the cheese: 'The colliers have found that it is not a crumbly cheese, and that is why it is so useful in Wales. You see, if they go down into the pit and take it with them it does not crumble and they are able to eat it.' At that time, traditional Caerphilly was 4cm thick and 38cm across, thereby yielding a good sized wedge to eat down the pit. Apparently, the miners were willing to pay more than twice the price for Caerphilly than a semi-skimmed milk cheese.

Poverty during the 19th century led farmers to skim their milk, churning the cream to make butter which was salted for the winter, and making a poor quality, brined cheese from the remaining milk. This was then sold at market within a couple of weeks for as little as 3p a pound. However, a full-cream Caerphilly would fetch 7p a pound. Ewe's milk was sometimes added to the skimmed cow's milk and this resulted in an altogether better and richer cheese. In her excellent book, *The First Principles of Good Cookery* (1867), Lady Llanover points out that ewe's milk was not generally used in England, but that ewe's cheeses made in Wales were excellent when fresh and as good as Parmesan when matured. According to Lady Llanover, 'The proportion for cheese should be one quart of ewe's milk to five quarts of cow's milk.' Goat's milk was traditionally used for cheesemaking until the 18th century. With a yield of more than two quarts a day, the Welsh goat could provide a nourishing, wholesome cheese which had a fine flavour and creamy texture, much superior to that made from skimmed cow's milk.

Many basic cheesemaking skills were lost during the First World War and, during the hard years that followed, the livelihood of many dairy farmers was only saved when the Milk Marketing Board was set up in 1933, thereby guaranteeing a regular income to milk suppliers.

However, it took another 40 years before the cheap price of land and a sense of adventure brought a new wave of cheesemakers to Wales, and one of the first of the 'new' cheeses produced was a Caerphilly made from a traditional recipe, in Ceredigion.

Start with contented cows and take their milk. Evening milk is richer than morning milk, so often a combination of the two is used. Allow the milk to stand in a vat overnight to ripen naturally and develop a good flavour. Then add a starter of lactic acid bacteria to speed up the souring process. This is not a harmful bacteria; it simply converts the milk sugar into lactic acid to encourage the milk to curdle. Now rennet is added and, together with the calcium in the milk, converts the protein, known as casein, into a junket-like mass called curd.

Next the curd is cut so that the whey can drain away. This must be done very slowly and carefully, with the aid of horizontal and vertical curd knives, to prevent the fat escaping. More moisture is lost by raking the curd, and it is also cooked by heating the water in the jacket of the cheese vat. The drained curd settles at the bottom of the vat where it is cut into blocks which are piled on top of one another and turned every ten minutes. You now have a dry, acid curd which, after about 50 minutes, is ready for milling. Chopped up into small granules, the milled curd has salt added before being packed into cheesecloth-lined moulds ready for pressing. It is pressed gently at first, with more pressure being applied each day until it is eventually transformed into a closely-knit cheese.

The cheese is then soaked in a salt brine which helps form a good rind and enhances the flavours. The drained cheeses are well dried before being left to mature. They are usually turned daily and maybe sold young (two weeks old), or as mature cheeses (two months old).

How to make Caerphilly Cheese

Brioche filled with Pencarreg Cheese

and Rhydlewis smoked Salmon

A delicious recipe from Beryl Tudhope who prepared this dish when she cooked at Tŷ Mawr Country Hotel, Brechfa. Beryl hasn't given the recipe for the brioche but she says that a herb bread, baked and shaped in a brioche tin, or individual cottage loaves would do fine.

1 Cut the top off each brioche and reserve for later use.

2 Scoop out the centre using a grapefruit knife. (Keep the crumbs and freeze for a treacle tart!)

3 Dice the Pencarreg cheese and the salmon and mix together. Add the herbs and place the mixture in the brioche shells.

4 Replace the lids and bake the brioches for 10 – 15 minutes at 400°F (200°C), Gas 6.

5 **For the dill sauce** beat the mustard, sugar and vinegar together, dribble in the oil and beat well. Mix in the dill and seasoning.

6 Serve the brioche with the dill sauce and garnish with fresh, snipped chives.

Ingredients

4 individual brioches, or small cottage loaves

225g (8oz) Pencarreg or Brie cheese

100g (4oz) Rhydlewis smoked salmon, cut into pieces

1 tablespoon chives, snipped

1 tablespoon parsley, chopped

Dill Sauce

2 tablespoons wholegrain mustard

1 tablespoon caster sugar

2 tablespoons tarragon vinegar

2 tablespoons light vegetable oil

2 tablespoons dried dill

¼ teaspoon each salt and pepper

Serves 4 as a starter

White Cheese Flan

Erddig, owned by the National Trust, is a late seventeenth-century house with eighteenth-century additions, and is probably the most evocative 'upstairs-downstairs' house in Britain. The range of outbuildings includes a kitchen, laundry, bakehouse, stables, sawmill, smithy and joiner's shop, while the state rooms display most of the original furniture and furnishings. The large, walled garden has been restored to its formal design, with Victorian parterre and yew walk. Erddig is also home to the national ivy collection. The restaurant is located in a restored haybarn off the main courtyard. This recipe was found in an old Welsh recipe book and adapted by Pat Bodymore, the Catering Manager at the National Trust Restaurant at Erddig, who introduced different Welsh cheeses and gave it an appropriate new name.

Ingredients

350g (12oz) pastry

225g (8oz) Caerphilly cheese, crumbled

100g (4oz) cream cheese

6 tablespoons Welsh cream

8 eggs

salt and pepper

4 tablespoons flour

2 tablespoons lemon juice

Serves 4

1 Pre-heat oven to 350°F [180°C], Gas 4.

2 Line a flan dish with shortcrust pastry and bake blind for 15 minutes.

3 Place the remaining ingredients in a large bowl and whisk until thick and creamy.

4 Pour into a flan case and return to oven for about 30 minutes, until set.

Glamorgan Sausages

Whether this recipe relates to the sausages that George Borrow describes in his book, *Wild Wales*, written in 1862, is hard to say. He remarked that, 'The breakfast was delicious, consisting of excellent tea, buttered toast and Glamorgan sausages, which I really think are not a whit inferior to those of Epping.' Today, this recipe is very popular with vegetarians and the cheese used is Caerphilly. But in Borrow's day it might well have been Glamorgan cheese made from the milk from Glamorgan cows, a breed much praised by Lady Llanover: 'The Glamorgan cows are magnificent animals, black, with a white stripe down the tail; excellent milkers.'

1 Mix together the breadcrumbs, leek, cheese, parsley, seasonings and mustard.

2 Beat together the two eggs and one yolk and use this to bind the mixture, adding a little milk if it is still too dry to hold together. Divide into twelve and roll into sausage shapes.

3 Chill in the fridge for 20 minutes.

4 Fry gently in oil until crisp and golden brown on all sides.

5 Serve with a fruity chutney.

Ingredients

150g (5oz) fresh, white breadcrumbs

1 small leek, finely chopped

75g (3oz) Caerphilly cheese, grated

1 tablespoon fresh parsley, chopped

salt and pepper

pinch of dry mustard

2 whole eggs

1 extra egg yolk

Serves 4

Caerphilly and Leek Pancake Dome

What could be more traditional to the Welsh than a stack of pancakes? Lloyd George was particularly partial to his pancakes for tea, but this recipe with a savoury filling might be more suitable for supper. The recipe is ideal for vegetarians.

Ingredients

For the batter

300ml (½ pint) milk

2 eggs

100g (4oz) plain flour

1 tablespoon melted butter

For the filling

a) 225g (8oz) Caerphilly cheese, grated

150ml (¼ pint) double cream

pinch of cayenne pepper

b) 1 large leek, chopped

100g (4oz) field mushrooms, chopped

25g (1oz) butter

Serves 6 – 8

1 Liquidize all the batter ingredients and leave to swell for 30 minutes.

2 To prepare the fillings, for filling a) grate the cheese and mix all but 50g (2oz) into the cream, and add the pepper.

3 For the second filling – fry the leek and mushrooms in the butter.

4 Make up 12 pancakes with the batter.

5 Layer the pancakes, interleaved alternately with the two fillings.

6 Place a pancake on top of the pile.

7 Sprinkle over the remaining cheese. Bake in a hot oven (450°F [230°C], Gas 8) for 15 minutes.

Powis Cheese Pudding

Powis Castle, owned by the National Trust, is a spectacular medieval fortress, originally built c.1200 by the Welsh Princes. It was subsequently adapted and embellished by generations of Herberts and Clives, who furnished the castle with a wealth of fine paintings and furniture. The world famous garden, overhung with enormous clipped yews, shelters rare and tender plants. Laid out under the influence of Italian and French styles, the garden retains its original lead statues, an orangery and an aviary on the terraces. The restaurant is located off the main courtyard of the castle. This dish was especially adapted for the National Trust Restaurant at Powis Castle by Diane Henry, the Catering Manager. It is made with two tangy, mature Welsh cheeses, Cosyn Coch and Hen Sir, and is both tasty and filling, served with crusty bread.

1. Set oven at 350°F [180°C], Gas 4.

2. Separate the eggs and beat the yolks lightly in a mixing bowl.

3. Warm the milk and add to the eggs, together with the butter and a pinch of mustard.

4. Mix well and add breadcrumbs and most of the cheese.

5. Season to taste.

6. Whip egg whites stiffly and fold into mixture.

7. Pour mixture into buttered pie dish and cover with the remaining grated cheese.

8. Cook for 30 – 40 minutes until well risen, golden brown and just set in the middle.

Ingredients

100g (4oz) Cosyn Coch

100g (4oz) Hen Sir

175g (6oz) fresh breadcrumbs

4 standard eggs

600ml (1 pint) milk

a good pinch of dry mustard

Serves 8

Welsh Rarebit

Perhaps this is the most famous of all Welsh recipes. Always a favourite in Wales, and known as 'roasted cheese' in medieval times, Welsh Rarebit has not always been a rich, savoury dish. It was once a recipe for using tough, poor-quality cheese, at a time when the cream from the top of the milk was used for butter and only skimmed milk for cheesemaking. Today, Welsh Rarebit should be prepared with one of the many Cheddar-type Welsh cheeses which are full of flavour.

Ingredients

225g (8oz) strong-flavoured Cheddar cheese

25g (1oz) butter, melted

1 tablespoon Worcester sauce

1 tablespoon mustard

1 tablespoon flour

4 tablespoons beer

4 slices toast

cayenne pepper

Serves 4

1 Grate the cheese and mix with the other ingredients to form a firm paste.

2 Spread over the four slices of toast, and grill gently until the topping is cooked through and golden brown.

Welsh Rarebit should be prepared with one of the many Cheddar-type Welsh cheeses which are full of flavour.

Merlin Cheesy Potato and Bacon Layer

A hearty dish of potatoes and bacon with Merlin cheese, a goat's cheese made by Gill and Ron Pateman on their farm in Ystrad Meurig.

1. Pre-heat the oven to 350°F [180°C], Gas 4. Part-boil the potatoes in lightly salted boiling water for 6 – 7 minutes.

2. Drain, cool slightly and slice thickly. Melt 25g (1oz) of butter and fry the onion until soft and golden.

3. Stir in the cheese, thyme, salt and pepper.

4. Butter an ovenproof dish and layer up the potatoes, onion mixture and bacon.

5. Pour the cream over and cook for 1½ hours in the oven until golden.

6. Serve hot with salad.

Ingredients

670g (1½lb) potatoes, peeled

40g (1½oz) butter

1 large onion, sliced

200g (7oz) Merlin mature mini, grated

1 tablespoon chopped, fresh thyme

salt and freshly ground pepper

8 rashers back bacon, rinded and cut into strips

250ml (8fl oz) single cream

Serves 4

Cheese has been produced on farms in Wales for centuries.

Welsh

It wasn't until the 1970s that traditional cheesemaking returned to rural Wales and in those early days, the skills were brought in by outsiders.

It was during a period of mountaineering in Switzerland that Dougal Campbell met up with a cheesemaker who taught him the art of producing holes in his cheese! Returning to Britain in 1976, Dougal gave up his career as a civil engineer, bought a farm in Lampeter and with the milk from one Jersey cow, tried to recreate that Swiss cheese. Alas, it simply didn't work, so Dougal adapted his skills and produced a farmhouse Cheddar which he called *Ty'n Grug*, after the farm. Inspired by nature and committed to the production of organic dairy products, Dougal then launched *Pencarreg*, a Brie-type cheese.

In 1977 when Leon Downey, a former principal viola player with the Halle orchestra, moved to a fifteen-acre smallholding in Llangloffan, near Fishguard, neighbours thought he was barmy. With little experience of farming, Leon and Joan began with one Jersey cow, and by delving in old agricultural books and conducting experiments on the farmhouse Aga. Today their *Llangloffen* cheese is in demand all over Britain.

Tony Craske first made cheese in 1980 when he had a glut of goat's milk. Tony and Pam Craske had returned from 25 years in Africa and Asia to buy a sixteenth-century hill farm at Mamhilad, near Abergavenny. The milkman couldn't get up the steep drive, so Tony bought some goats in order that their three children could enjoy their breakfast cereal as usual! With a background as an industrial chemist and a lifetime spent in the paint industry, Tony naturally fell into making a soft goat's cheese! Thirty years on, the Craske family now produce a range of cheeses, which they sell mainly to supermarkets. Ranging from *Pant-ysgawen*, their original soft goat's cheese, to washed rind *St David's*, traditional Caerphilly and a most successful range of milled cheeses such as: *St. Illtyd*, a Cheddar-type cheese with garlic, wine and herbs; *Y Fenni*, a Cheddar with mustard seed and ale; and *Brecon Blue*, a goat's and cow's milk blue cheese.

Cheesemakers from Holland have brought their skills to cheesemaking in Wales, too. *Teifi Farmhouse Cheese* made by Patrice and John Savage, is available in plain, garlic, garlic and onion, celery, nettle, sweet pepper, chives, laverbread, mustard and cumin seed. The flavour is nutty and rich when young but, as it matures, *Teifi* takes on a sweet, dense flavour.

Cheese

Their *Celtic Promise*, a washed rind cheese has a superb mature flavour.

It was the introduction of milk quotas in 1984, when so many dairy farms sought alternative ways to use up their milk supplies and supplement farm incomes that cheesemaking really took off in Wales. It was at this time that Thelma Adams decided to make a traditional Caerphilly, which she called *Caws Cenarth* on her farm at Pontseli, near Boncath. Thelma worked tirelessly to promote Welsh cheesemaking and encourage others, and today she is part of a cheese marketing company which encompasses the very best of Welsh cheeses called Cheeses from Wales. See www.cheesesfromwales.co.uk.

Members include small on-farm producers through to larger, creamery-scale operators. This superb range of cheeses includes varieties derived from cow, goat and sheep's milk, both pasteurised and unpasteurised.

Look out for.....

Cheddar from the **Blaenafon Cheddar Company** which was established in 2007 in the World Heritage town of Blaenafon in south Wales.

Caerfai Organic, a family-run business owned by Wyn and Chris Evans and located on a coastal farm near St Davids, Pembrokeshire.

Colliers Powerful Cheddar, made by Faryrefields Foods which was formed in 1982.

Hafod made by Sam and Rachel Holden in Ceredigion since 2007 using raw milk from the farms' 65 Ayrshire cows.

Llanboidy made within a small family business over the past 30 years.

Gorwydd Caerphilly, produced by Tod Trethowan.

Merlin Goat's cheeses, made in the mountain village of Pontrhydgroes in mid Wales by Gill Pateman.

Caws Mynydd Du, a sheeps milk cheese produced on the farm at the foot of the Black Mountains.

Nantybwla Farmhouse Caerphilly, an unpasteurised cheese made from pedigree Jersey and Holstein cattle.

Pant Mawr Farmhouse cheese, established in 1983 by the Jennings family.

Cheddar from the **Pembrokeshire Cheese Company**.

Sanclêr Organic, an organic yoghurt cheese which was developed over 10 years.

And last, but not least, the highly successful **Snowdonia Cheese Company** whose cheese is sold nationwide.

Baking

Anglesey Shortbread

11

Baking

At the beginning of the last century, a Welsh housewife might expect to spend one whole day a week baking.

She would prepare a huge amount of dough first thing in the morning and then, with the oven lit, bake enough loaves to feed the family for the entire week. Once the bread was baked and the temperature dropped, tarts, buns and *bara brith* – a fruit loaf – was cooked. Finally, a rice pudding would enjoy the fading heat.

Much bread would also have been baked in the large oven of a village bakery. These ovens were made of bricks and heated by means of a fire. Once hot, the ashes were raked out, the bread put in, and the oven door sealed with clay. A fine example of a faggot oven is still in use at the Museum of Welsh Life in St Fagans, near Cardiff.

Although wheat is now the most important grain for baking in Wales, up until the end of the 19th century it was oats that played the most important part in the rural diet. Geraldus Cambrensis, during his tour of Wales in 1188, noted that ' ... almost all the people live upon the produce of their herds, with

oats, milk, cheese and butter'. And during the 19th century Lady Llanover confirmed, 'The preparation of oatmeal is particularly well understood in Wales, as well as in Scotland ... Next to bread and good water, oatmeal may be considered as one of the first necessaries of life to a rural population ...' Although we think of oatcakes as a Scottish speciality, these were part of the Welsh daily diet too – but rolled out very large and very thin, a traditional Welsh oatcake used to be the size of a dinner plate.

Before ovens were readily available, a variety of little cakes and scones were cooked in a metal box called a Dutch oven, which sat in the embers of an open fire. The following is Lady Llanover's recipe for *Teisen Frau Gwent a Morgannwg*, the cakes eaten in south-east Wales:

Rubbing six ounces of butter in one pound of flour and two teaspoonfuls of sugar made into a stiff dough

with new milk, or sheep's milk cream, roll it out half an inch thick, and cut to size required; bake on a bake-stone or before the fire in a Dutch oven.

Animal lard was popular in home baking, and one of the main sources of lard was the flead of a pig, the inner fatty membrane surrounding the kidneys and loin. Flead cakes were made until quite recently by beating together flead, flour and salt. These cakes were the ancestors of lardy cakes and were sold at fairs.

Fairings is the name given to food, drink and goods available at the many country fairs that used to take place throughout Wales. Often the autumn and spring fairs were hiring fairs, where labourers sought work. Particular pies and cakes were associated with some of the fairs: for example, at Templeton Fair, little lamb and currant pies, known as Katt Pies after St. Katherine, were popular.

Bara Brith

Bara brith literally means 'speckled bread', a loaf dotted with mixed fruit and spice. Traditionally, it would have been made with the remains of the yeast bread dough after a day's baking, but this simple recipe makes a delicious bara brith.

Ingredients

450g (1lb) mixed raisins, sultanas and currants

300ml (½ pint) cold tea

2 tablespoons marmalade

1 egg, beaten

2 tablespoons soft brown sugar

1 teaspoon mixed spice

450g (1lb) self-raising flour

honey to glaze

1 Soak the fruit overnight in the tea.

2 Next day, mix in the marmalade, egg, sugar, spice and flour. Spoon into a greased 900g (2lb) loaf tin and bake in a warm oven (325ºF [170ºC], Gas 3) for 1¾ hours, or until the centre is cooked through.

3 Check from time to time to see that the top doesn't brown too much, and cover with a sheet of foil if necessary.

4 Once cooked, leave the bara brith to stand for 5 minutes, then remove from the tin and place on a cooling tray, brush honey over the top to glaze.

Welsh Pan or Pot Bread

Imagine, if you can, making a loaf of bread baked in a saucepan. This is how, according to an old recipe.

1 Take three pounds and a half of brown flour, put it to rise with about two tablespoons of barm (yeast) and when risen, mix it and knead it in the usual manner.

2 Then put it into an iron pot or thick earthen pan, and turn it topsy-turvy on a flat stone, which should be placed on the ground in the middle of a heap of hot embers, made by burning wood, peat or turf.

3 Cover the pot or pan entirely over with hot embers, leave it to bake, and when the ashes are cold take it out.

4 This mode of baking produces most excellent bread.

Teisennau Berffro

(Anglesey Shortbread)

A biscuit recipe from Aberffraw, Anglesey where the Princes of Gwynedd held court during the Middle Ages. Small queen scallop shells are used to shape the biscuits called *Teisennau Berffro*, an abbreviated form of the place-name Aberffraw.

1 Rub the butter into the flour until the mixture resembles fine breadcrumbs.

2 Stir in the sugar. Using your fingertips, press the mixture together and knead to a smooth, pliable paste.

3 Roll out fairly thinly on a well-floured board and cut into 5cm (2 inch) circles.

4 Using the tip of a sharp-bladed knife, mark each with a scallop-shell pattern.

5 Bake in a moderately hot oven (375°F [190°C] Gas 5) for about 10 minutes, until the biscuits turn a pale, golden colour.

6 Cool on the baking tray and when cold, sprinkle lavishly with caster sugar.

7 Store in an airtight tin for up to a week.

Ingredients

175g (6oz) butter

225g (8oz) flour

100g (4oz) caster sugar, plus extra for dredging

Teisen Lap

A popular recipe in the south Wales mining valleys, this 'moist' cake would have been eaten by miners at lunch time. It didn't crumble or make them too thirsty, so it was the ideal 'filler' to pack into their lunch tins and take down the pit. Babs Meredith, who understands the baking properties of buttermilk, created this recipe in Llanidloes.

Ingredients

225g (8oz) plain flour

1 teaspoon baking powder

a pinch of salt

a pinch of grated nutmeg

100g (4oz) Welsh butter

75g (3oz) caster sugar

100g (4oz) sultanas

2 eggs, size 3, beaten

150ml (¼ pint) buttermilk

1 Sieve the flour, baking powder, salt and nutmeg into a bowl.

2 Rub in the butter, then add the sugar, fruit and eggs. Add the buttermilk gradually, beating with a wooden spoon, until you have a mixture soft enough to drop, albeit reluctantly, from the spoon.

3 Bake in a greased and lined, 22cm (9 inch) round sponge tin at 350ºF [180°C], Gas 4 for 30 – 40 minutes until golden brown and well risen.

This 'moist' cake would have been eaten by miners at lunch time.

Spiced Honey Loaf

Although this is a traditional Welsh recipe, I first tasted spiced honey loaf during holidays spent in Brittany. As children we used to nibble pain d'epices, bread of spices, on the beach, quite unaware of the Celtic connection.

1 Set the oven to 325ºF [160ºC], Gas 3.

2 Stir the honey into the boiling water.

3 Oil and flour a 900g (2lb) loaf tin.

4 Sieve the flour and salt, and add the sugar and spice. Using a wooden spoon, add the melted honey and water, beating until bubbles appear.

5 Stir in the baking powder and bicarbonate of soda.

6 Pour the mixture into the bread tin and bake for an hour or until a skewer inserted into the loaf comes out clean, with no trace of dough adhering to it.

7 Serve the loaf warm or cold, as it is or spread with butter or cream cheese.

Ingredients

100g (4oz) or 4 level tablespoons runny honey

150ml (5fl oz) boiling water

225g (8oz) plain flour

pinch of salt

100g (4oz) caster sugar

1 teaspoon mixed spice

1 teaspoon ground ginger

1 level teaspoon bicarbonate of soda

1 level teaspoon baking powder

The Bakestone

Welsh cakes

12

The Bake

The bakestone (*planc* or *maen* in Welsh) still plays an important part in everyday life. Oatcakes, Welsh cakes, tinker's cakes, pancakes, even loaves of bread: traditionally, all were cooked on the griddle, and with a degree of skill too.

If you go to Swansea Market you can buy *bara planc* or griddle bread, and there is a baker in Fishguard who also prepares it. In his autobiographical study, *Across the Straits* (1973), Kyffin Williams, the famous Welsh artist who lived on Anglesey, had this to say about the *crempog* teas served in local farms:

We used to visit farms for crempog teas and I used to eye the huge pot of melted butter, in which lurked the small round pancakes, with apprehension. I knew I could never eat enough to satisfy the farmer's wife, and always when I had consumed about six I could take no more. Unfortunately one's manhood was judged by one's capacity to down a vast number of crempogau and I always failed abysmally in the eyes of the parish, 'Well, well, you are no good,' complained one old body. 'Your father Master Johnny could do twenty and your grandfather twenty-four.' I was humiliated and hardly a member of the rector's family any more. 'Dduw, Master John, only six? Well, well, you're hopeless.' There would be laughter and cheerful goodbyes, but I crept away, a six-crempog boy.

Welsh Cakes

These little cakes are cooked on a bakestone or *maen*, that is the stone on which they are griddled. Although bakestones are found in all the Celtic countries, only in Wales do we griddle these sweet cakes. A heavy frying pan works well, but take care not to let the sugar in your Welsh cakes burn.

Ingredients

225g (8oz) self-raising flour

pinch of salt

100g (4oz) mixed butter and lard

75g (3oz) caster sugar

75g (3oz) currants

½ teaspoon mixed spice

1 teaspoon honey

1 medium egg, beaten

1 In a bowl, rub the fats into the flour until the mixture resembles breadcrumbs.

2 Stir in the sugar, currants, mixed spice and honey. Add the beaten egg and mix to form a firm dough.

3 On a floured board, roll or pat out the mixture until about 2cm (½ inch) thick.

4 Cut into 6cm (2½ inch) discs and griddle over medium heat until golden brown on both sides.

5 Dust the Welsh cakes with caster sugar and eat immediately or store in an airtight tin.

A heavy frying pan works well, but take care not to let the sugar in your Welsh cakes burn.

Rhubarb Tarten Planc with Strawberry and Elderflower Sauce

This recipe is Celtic to the core. *Tarten planc* is a pastry tart baked on a griddle or *planc*. It is, in effect, a fruit turnover and has a very special flavour due to the slow cooking of the pastry on the direct heat of the griddle. But beware! Turning over your tart on the griddle, so as to ensure that both sides are equally brown and that the filling remains in the middle, is an art!

1 Cook the rhubarb in the orange juice (ideally, in a microwave) until just tender but still holding its shape. Sweeten with honey. Leave to cool.

2 Make up the pastry as for shortbread by rubbing the butter into the mixed plain and wholemeal flour, adding just enough water to make a firm dough.

3 Leave to rest for an hour before rolling out into discs with a 7.5cm (3 inch) pastry cutter.

4 Place 1 tablespoon of the rhubarb on half of the discs and cover with the remaining discs, sealing the edges with a little water. Press the discs together firmly at the edges.

5 Bake on a griddle over moderate heat, turning carefully to cook both sides. Serve the tarts warm, dredged with caster sugar and surrounded by a spoonful of sauce.

Ingredients

For the pastry

150g (6oz) flour (a mixture of plain white and wholemeal)

75g (3oz) butter

pinch of salt

water to mix

For the filling

450g (1lb) rhubarb, sliced (gooseberries could also be used)

juice of half an orange

honey to taste

For the sauce

225g (8oz) of fresh strawberries liquidised with a tablespoon of elderflower cordial. Sieve the puree and sweeten to taste.

Tinker's Cakes

It is romantic to think that these little griddle cakes were made for travelling tinkers. In rural areas, the arrival of a tinker would call for some sort of celebration where, with luck, he would share all the gossip and news he had collected on his travels. And what better way to persuade him to part with all his news, than a plate of tinker's cakes.

Ingredients

225g (8oz) self-raising flour

pinch of salt

100g (4oz) butter

75g (3oz) soft brown sugar

½ teaspoon cinnamon

1 medium cooking apple

1 small egg, beaten

1 Place the flour and salt into a large bowl and rub in the butter until the mixture resembles fine breadcrumbs.

2 Add the sugar and cinnamon. Peel the apple and grate it into the mixture, stirring to prevent the flesh from turning brown.

3 Add the beaten egg to make a firm dough. On a floured board, roll or pat the dough out to about 0.5cm (¼ inch) thick. Either cut into 5cm (2 inch) discs with a pastry cutter or into larger 10cm (4 inch) circles, which are more difficult to deal with, but more fun to serve.

4 Heat the griddle or heavy-based frying pan and cook the tinker's cakes gently for about 3 minutes on each side.

5 Serve warm from the griddle, well sprinkled with caster sugar. Cut the larger discs into wedges.

Pikelets

Welsh pancakes are thick, and pikelets are even thicker! When Eleri Davies of Pentre Farm, Lampeter, has guests at the farmhouse she may have to cook for as many as ten people. When serving pikelets, she simply makes up the batter during the meal and griddles the little pancakes at the very last minute so that they fly hot from the pan to the plate, and are served with ice cream and a fruit sauce.

1 In a food processor or liquidiser, blend all the ingredients into a thick batter.

2 Heat a griddle and drop on tablespoonfuls of the mixture. Cook through on both sides so that they begin to curl at the edges.

3 Roll up the cooked pikelets, stack on a plate and dredge with brown sugar.

4 Serve with ice cream and stewed fresh fruit, or a syrup or chocolate sauce.

Ingredients

225g (8oz) plain flour

450ml (16fl oz) milk

4 eggs

75g (3oz) melted butter

1 teaspoon caster sugar

Griddle the little pancakes at the very last minute so that they fly hot from the pan to the plate.

Oatcakes

The making of oatmeal cakes was something of an art, at least according to Lady Llanover who observed that:

'The rolling-pin must not be used in making these cakes, all must be done with the hand, and they must be flattened and worked round and round with the hand until they are almost as thin as a wafer. Make a stiff paste with oatmeal and water or skim milk; then form it into balls with the hand about the size of small eggs; then shape with the hand round and round to the size of a small cheese-plate or large saucer; when one oat-cake is formed the right shape and thickness, turn it and shake dry oatmeal all over it; then take another, put it in the middle of the oat-cake you have made, and form that in the same manner upon the first made; when well tempered, turn it, and shake dry oatmeal all over it, and proceed in the same way until you have got eighteen oat-cakes one on the other. When dry enough to put on the bakestone (heated to the required point which practice alone can teach), bake them one at a time; have a clean cloth folded to the proper shape, and press the cake down flat on the bake-stone, where it should remain until it is of a nice light brown colour.'

Lady Llanover, *The First Principles of Good Cookery* (1867).

Being a beginner in the art of making oatcakes, I must admit to cheating a little. My oatcakes are made infinitely easier to handle by mixing the oatmeal with an equal quantity of wholewheat flour and binding the mixture with a higher proportion of fat.

1 In a large bowl, mix the oatmeal, flour, salt and bicarbonate of soda.

2 Rub in the fat, using your fingertips. Mix to a soft but not sticky dough with the cold water.

3 On a board, dusted with wholewheat flour, roll out to a large circle about 25cm (10 inch) in diameter, using only half the dough.

4 Either cut the dough into circles using a pastry cutter, or leave as one large disc, dividing it into eight portions, similar to shortbread.

5 Bake in the oven (325ºF [160ºC], Gas 3) for about 20 minutes until pale gold, or griddle over a medium heat, turning once after a few minutes in order to brown both sides.

Ingredients

175g (6oz) medium oatmeal

175g (6oz) wholemeal flour

1 teaspoon salt

¼ teaspoon bicarbonate of soda

75g (3oz) butter, margarine or bacon fat

about 2 tablespoons cold water

The rolling-pin must not be used in making these cakes, all must be done with the hand.

Puddings and other Sweet Delicacies

Monmouth Pudding

13

Puddings and Delicacies

Traditionally, Welsh puddings have always been based on milk or fruit, so it is not surprising that rice pudding was for the past century the most highly-esteemed Sunday pudding.

other Sweet

Besides, when the roast occupies the top half of the oven, how convenient to use the lower, cooler shelf for the rice pud. Ground nutmeg or a bay leaf is sometimes added, or even a handful of sultanas for sweetness.

Other milk puddings, such as Snowdonia or Monmouth pudding, combining breadcrumbs, egg and butter are also popular in Wales, and are creamy-tasting and inexpensive. Junket or curd cakes, using full-fat milk fresh from the cow, are quite delicious, as are pancakes made with buttermilk for a touch of sharpness, and all rich creamy desserts such as syllabubs and fruit fools.

Welsh country folk were well used to combing hedgerows, fields and woodlands for wild fruit and flowers. Lavender or elderflower would be used to flavour many dishes; the plum and apple harvest would also be eagerly awaited, for even a simple pie made from windfall apples, baked on an enamel plate, has always been a family favourite.

Dried fruits mixed with spices have been enjoyed in Wales ever since the Crusaders returned from the Holy Land, bringing with them such exotic tastes as cinnamon, ginger, apricots, lemons, sultanas and almonds.

In recent years, following the introduction of milk quotas, dairy farmers have turned their milk into alternative products such as ice cream made with nothing but natural ingredients: full-fat milk, double cream and flavoured with nuts, fruit or local honey. Such creamy ices are heaven. Generally speaking, ice cream is a local product and each producer distributes only within the compass of a few hilly miles. Visitors, therefore, are advised to carry out their own ice cream survey, as they travel through Wales, in order to decide which they like best!

After the plates had been polished clean with bread, the pudding came out, and let me tell you my mother's pudding would make you hold your breath to eat. Sometimes it was a pie or stewed fruit with thick cream from the farm that morning, but whatever it was, it was always good.

Richard Llewellyn, *How Green Was My Valley* (1939).

Snowdon Pudding

It is said that Eliza Acton, the famous nineteenth-century cook, ate this pudding at the Pen-y-groes Hotel not too far from the foot of Snowdon, well over a hundred years ago! It is a typical suet pudding, rich and filling, but with some delicious extra ingredients and a sauce with an unforgettable flavour.

Ingredients

100g (4oz) vegetarian suet

100g (4oz) white breadcrumbs

1 tablespoon cornflour or ground rice

pinch of salt

finely grated rind of 1 lemon

2 tablespoons lemon or orange marmalade

3 tablespoons brown sugar

3 well-beaten eggs

3 tablespoons seedless raisins

a little butter

Serves 6

1 Grease a 15cm (6 inch) pudding basin with the butter and then press as many raisins as will stick on the inner side of the basin.

2 Mix the suet, breadcrumbs, cornflour and salt, then add the grated lemon rind, marmalade and sugar. Add the beaten eggs and any remaining raisins.

3 Carefully spoon the mixture into the basin.

4 Cover and steam for 50 – 60 minutes, or microwave on High for 5 minutes.

5 Turn out onto a warm plate and serve with the wine sauce.

Wine Sauce

2 tablespoons granulated sugar

½ lemon rind in one piece

2 tablespoons water

1 teaspoon cornflour

1 tablespoon butter

150ml (¼ pint) Madeira, sweet sherry, Marsala or home-made sweet wine

1 Boil the sugar, lemon rind and water for 15 minutes and then remove the rind.

2 Mix the cornflour into the butter, and stir into the syrup. Add the wine and let it simmer for a few minutes to thicken.

3 Serve in a small jug with the steaming hot pudding.

Sunday Rice Pudding

A bay leaf and some sweet, plump raisins give Welsh rice pudding that little extra which makes it so special. Traditionally served for Sunday lunch, a rich, creamy, baked rice pudding would follow the roast. In Yorkshire there was always a batter pudding tucked away on the cooler shelf under the roasting joint, and in Wales, for the same economic reason, there was a rice pudding. And if the family felt too full to tackle the rice pudding at lunch, then it was saved for tea and served as a treat.

1 Wash the rice and soak in cold water for 15 minutes.

2 Grease a 1.2 litre (2 pint) shallow, ovenproof dish, place the bay leaf in the bottom and sprinkle in the drained rice. Add the sugar, raisins, salt, milk and butter. Grate the nutmeg over the surface.

3 Cook the pudding in a warm oven (325°F [170°C], Gas 3) for 2 – 2 ½ hours, adding a little more milk if the pudding begins to look dry, until the rice grains are soft and the top is golden brown.

4 Serve with lashings of thick, double cream.

Ingredients

50g (2oz) short grain rice

1 bay leaf

50g (2oz) caster sugar

50g (2oz) raisins or currants

pinch of salt

600ml (1 pint) full cream milk

small knob of butter

nutmeg, freshly grated

Serves 4

A bay leaf and some sweet, plump raisins give Welsh rice pudding that little extra which makes it so special.

Welsh Blackberry and Apple Pudding

Here is a recipe for a traditional Welsh blackberry and apple pudding. Bowls of steaming pudding might well have been served to hungry harvesters at the end of a busy day in the fields. A hearty dish, full of goodness!

Ingredients

450g (1lb) cooking apples, peeled, cored and sliced

a handful of freshly picked blackberries

4 tablespoons water

100g (4oz) granulated sugar

4 cloves

35g (1½oz) butter

50g (2oz) flour

450ml (15fl oz) milk

25g (1oz) caster sugar

2 eggs, separated

a few drops of vanilla essence

Serves 4

1 In a saucepan containing the water, place the apples, granulated sugar and cloves. Cook the apples until tender, adding the blackberries for the last 5 minutes.

2 Remove the cloves and place the apple mixture in a well-buttered, oven-proof dish.

3 Melt the butter in a saucepan, stir in the flour and gradually add the milk. Bring slowly to the boil, stirring constantly. Remove from the heat, add the caster sugar, egg yolks and vanilla essence, and mix thoroughly.

4 Whisk the egg whites until stiff. Fold into the sauce and pour over the blackberries and apples.

5 Bake for 45 minutes in a moderately hot oven (400°F [200°C], Gas 6), until risen and crisp.

6 Serve hot with cream or custard.

If your apples bloom in March
In rain you'll for them search;
If apples bloom in April
When then they'll be plentiful;
If apples bloom in May
You may eat them night and day.

Anon

Monmouth Pudding

Monmouth Pudding is a direct descendant of Queen of Puddings and revels in the fact that it is easy and economical to produce. The addition of fresh fruit, instead of jam, and a crisp meringue topping has done wonders for the image of Monmouth Pudding!

1 Add the lemon rind, sugar and butter to the milk and bring to the boil.

2 Pour the mixture over the breadcrumbs and leave to stand for 15 minutes.

3 Stir the egg yolks into the cooled bread mixture and spoon into one large or four small ramekin dishes.

4 Spread a layer of jam or some fresh fruit over the top and cover with meringue.

Ingredients

450ml (15fl oz) full cream milk

grated rind of 1 lemon

2 tablespoons caster sugar

25g (1oz) butter

175g (6oz) fresh, white breadcrumbs

3 egg yolks

4 – 5 tablespoons raspberry jam or 100g (4oz) fresh fruit, strawberries, cherries, etc.

Serves 4

1 To prepare the meringue topping, whisk the egg whites until stiff, fold in the sugar and swirl the meringue on top of the ramekins.

2 Either place the ramekins into a moderately hot oven (400°F [200°C], Gas 6) for 10 minutes to crisp, or bake in a slow oven (300°F [150°C], Gas 2) until the meringue is crisp and golden brown.

3 Allow about 15 minutes if using ramekins for each individual pudding and 30 minutes for a large dish.

For the meringue topping

3 egg whites

6 tablespoons caster sugar

Plum and Hazelnut Cobbler

This is a most satisfactory pudding; filling, and with lots of fruity flavour. The cobbler or scone topping could be used over any stewed fruit.

Ingredients

900g (2lbs) stewed plums, stoned

sugar to taste

a good pinch of cinnamon

For the cobbler

225g (8oz) self-raising flour

50g (2oz) hazelnuts, toasted and skinned

50g (2oz) butter

2 tablespoons caster sugar

1 egg, and milk to mix

Serves 4

1 Arrange the fruit in the bottom of a large gratin dish.

2 In a processor or large bowl, sift the flour with a pinch of salt, and rub in the butter. Add the nuts and sugar, blend in the egg and enough milk to ensure a dropping consistency.

3 Dollop the cobbler mixture around the top of the fruit and bake at once (375°F [190°C], Gas 5) for 30 minutes, or until crisp.

4 Serve with crème fraîche.

Dollop the cobbler mixture around the top of the fruit and bake for 30 minutes.

Welsh cakes with Apples, Caerphilly Cream and Red Berry Sauce

1 Rub the fats into the flour. Add the sugar, currants, mixed spice and honey. Mix to a firm dough with the beaten egg. Roll or pat out the mixture until about 1cm (½ inch) thick.

2 Cut into 6cm (2½ inch) discs and griddle over medium heat until golden on both sides.

3 To serve, split each Welsh cake and place one thin disc in the centre of a pretty plate. Spread over a layer of the creamed Caerphilly, followed by a good spoonful of apple. Place the remaining Welsh cake disc, at an angle, on top of the apple and pour the red berry sauce around. Dust well with icing sugar.

Ingredients

For the Welsh cakes

225g (8oz) self-raising flour

100g (4oz) mixed butter and lard

75g (3oz) caster sugar

75g (3oz) currants

½ teaspoon mixed spice

1 teaspoon honey

1 medium egg, beaten

For the cheese layer

Mix together 100g (4oz) of grated Caerphilly cheese and 6 tablespoons of single cream.

For the apple layer

Cook 2 peeled, cored and diced cooking apples gently, with 25g (1oz) butter and a pinch of spice, until soft and pulpy. Sweeten to taste with 2 tablespoons of honey.

For the red berry sauce

Mix together 150g (5oz) blackberries, whinberries, raspberries or fresh currants with 4 tablespoons of water and 2 tablespoons of caster sugar. Simmer gently until thick and then sieve.

Siot

The original recipe for Siot was based on a mixture of oatcakes crumbled in buttermilk, and many people in Wales remember eating Siot as children. This recipe has a modern twist and the Scots may call this *Athol brose* and claim it as their own – not so, our Celtic cousins!

Ingredients

100g (4oz) medium oatmeal

1 tablespoon heather honey

1 tablespoon caster sugar

1 tablespoon fresh lemon juice

225g (8oz) summer fruit, such as strawberries or raspberries

300ml (½ pint) Greek-style yoghurt

1 Soak all but a spoonful of the oatmeal in cold water overnight. The oatmeal will absorb about twice its volume in water.

2 Next day, strain off any excess water. Place the creamy oatmeal into a bowl and stir in the honey, caster sugar and lemon juice. Add the yoghurt and taste for sweetness.

3 Chop the fruit into bite-sized pieces and arrange in the bottom of one large or six individual glass dishes.

4 Spoon over the oatmeal cream.

5 Toast the remaining oatmeal until brown and nutty, either in a dry frying pan or under the grill, or bake in the oven for 10 minutes.

6 Sprinkle a dusting of toasted oatmeal on top.

Many people in Wales remember eating Siot as children.

Lavender Syllabub

The earliest syllabubs were made by mixing milk, warm from the cow, with ale or cider. After a short time, a curd formed on top of the whey. This, however, posed a practical problem, for the dish had to be partly eaten and partly drunk. In time, wine was used in place of ale, and cream instead of milk. Indeed, by the 18th century, the proportion of cream was increased and the wine reduced, thereby ensuring that the final mixture was uniformly thick and of a delicious lightness and delicacy of flavour.

1 Boil the water and pour onto the lavender. Leave to infuse for 20 minutes.

2 Strain the lavender water and pour into a small saucepan. Add the sugar and bring the syrup to the boil. Continue boiling for 1 minute.

3 Cool the syrup, pour into a deep bowl, and add the lemon juice and wine.

4 Using a balloon or hand-held electric whisk, slowly add the cream to the wine mixture.

5 Continue to whisk hard until the mixture thickens to a soft peak.

6 Spoon into glasses and stand in a cool place until required. (Choose a cool larder in preference to a fridge.)

7 Serve with plain, crisp biscuits.

Ingredients

120ml (4fl oz) water

4 large heads of lavender, or 1 tablespoon dried lavender

100g (4oz) caster sugar

juice of ½ lemon

350ml (12fl oz) double cream

3 tablespoons of fruity, dry white Welsh wine

Honey and Lemon Ice Cream

Ingredients

300ml (½ pint) double cream

300ml (½ pint) plain yoghurt

2 unwaxed lemons, grated rind and squeezed juice

2 tablespoons honey, melted or runny

sugar to taste

1. Whisk the cream until it has the same thick consistency as the yoghurt.

2. Mix the cream, yoghurt, lemon rind and juice, honey and sugar together and stir to ensure the ingredients are thoroughly blended.

3. Transfer to a plastic container. Freeze the ice cream until firm. Serve with honey shortbread.

Honey Shortbread

Ingredients

225g (8oz) plain flour

100g (4oz) slightly salted butter

2 tablespoons honey

1 small egg, beaten

icing sugar

a few drops of rosewater

1. Rub the butter into the flour until it looks like breadcrumbs.

2. Stir in the honey and egg, and press the mixture together to form a dough.

3. Roll out into a long sausage shape the width of a finger, and cut into 2.5cm (1 inch) lengths. Curl slightly and arrange on a baking sheet.

4. Bake at 350°F (180°C), Gas 4 for 15 minutes until it begins to brown.

5. Leave the shortbread to cool, before dredging with icing sugar and sprinkling with a few drops of rosewater.

Plygain Toffee

The word *plygain* refers to the crow of a cock, the first sign of dawn, the time when traditional Welsh carols or chants used to be sung on Christmas morning. Alas, this tradition only persists in a few rural communities today. In order to keep the family going through the long Christmas Eve night, social events such as making treacle toffee, called *cyflaith*, helped to pass the time. Take great care when making toffee, for it has the ability to retain its heat.

1 Combine all the ingredients in a large pan over gentle heat. When the sugar has completely dissolved, turn up the heat and boil hard for about 20 minutes.

2 To test the toffee, drop a little into a cup of cold water: if it hardens immediately, then the toffee is ready.

3 Pour the toffee onto a buttered surface (a marble slab is best) and allow to cool a little.

4 Butter your hands, and as soon as you can touch the toffee, start to pull it into long strands. At this stage the colour turns golden. Keep working the toffee until it becomes firm.

5 Cut into small chunks.

Ingredients

450g (1lb) black treacle

225g (8oz) soft brown sugar

a good knob of butter

½ teaspoon vinegar

In our atomized and secular culture of today we are incapable of celebrating any festival in a community fashion and our Christmas festivities have changed accordingly. Perhaps the most striking fact of all is that many people have so forgotten the old Christmas of the plygain, the squirrel-hunting, the toffee-making, the visiting and the local football match as to believe that the scenes depicted on our Christmas cards really represent an old-fashioned Christmas.

Trefor M. Owen, *Welsh Folk Customs* (1968).

Country Drinks

Honeyed Pears with Mead

14

Country D

Country wines have been just as much a part of rural Welsh life as bacon curing and the making of fruit pies and tarts.

Many households made a variety of wines from hedgerow and other fruits – fragrant elderberry or gooseberry, blackberry or blackcurrant – and this rewarding hobby is still practised today. Ready in as little as six weeks, these sometimes potent wines were used medicinally as a pick-me-up, or sometimes served, like Madeira, with a cake at tea time.

It was the Romans who first introduced viniculture to Wales (the largest Roman vineyard in Britain was established in the Vale of Glamorgan) and some of those original, sunny, south-facing slopes are used again today to grow crops of grapes for wine. Viniculture continued up to the medieval period, and is associated in particular with the churches and monasteries established by the Normans. The twelfth-century historian Geraldus Cambrensis (Gerald of Wales) spoke of vines being grown in Wales on stakes or trellises, and of excellent vines grown at the monastery of

Caerleon-upon-Usk. In 1186 the Cistercian abbey of Margam in West Glamorgan is known to have established a good vineyard. A vineyard also graced the home of the fourteenth-century Welsh leader, Owain Glyndŵr.

The success of the Plantagenets in France almost put paid to the production of wines in Britain. Wines from French vineyards became not only fashionable, but also cheaper than those produced in Britain. As a consequence, the cultivation of vineyards declined to the level where it became merely a hobby for the wealthy. The last of the large-scale private vineyards was located on the Marquess of Bute's estate at Castell Coch, but this was abandoned during the First World War. Following the demise of this vineyard, an article published in *Punch* spoke of the mediocre quality of the wine, saying, 'It would take four men to drink this wine, the victim (a Welshman) and three Englishmen, two to hold him down and one to pour it down the Welshman's throat!'

Although interest in wine production increased after the Second World War, it was not until the 1970s that any serious attempts were made to re-establish viniculture in the once thriving wine-producing areas of south Wales.

However, winemaking in Wales is not and never will be easy. The weather sees to that. During the growing season, flowering, bud burst, fruit set and general swelling of the grapes all need to go according to plan. But if the plan is upset by a hail storm or a late frost, a bout of fungal disease or mildew brought about by excessive rain, attacks from birds or hares, not to mention wasps, the crop is a loser. And that is before Customs and Excise officers get involved! But despite the problems, there are now over a dozen vineyards in Wales, all in the south, with some of the wines achieving a standard of quality equal to any made in the British Isles. The grapes used are mainly hybrid Alsace-type, such as Madeleine Angevine, Seyval Blanc, Reichensteiner, Leon Millot and Triomphe d'Alsace, which are able to withstand the Welsh climate. Welsh wines are mainly light, dry and fruity in character, and many of the vineyards welcome visitors and offer wine tasting sessions.

Mother made wine from cowslips, parsnips, elderberry, elderflower, damson and gorse flower. The gorse petals were picked when the sun beat fiercely upon them and taken hurriedly home and put into a vat. The gorseflower wine left no hangover but the effect of a few glasses was to make one feel Olympian, one of the Gods.

James Williams, *Give Me Yesterday* (1971).

Elderberry Cordial

A soothing drink for colds and sore throats in winter, or a refreshing summer drink when mixed with soda, ice and lemon.

Ingredients

900g (2lbs) elderberries, weighed after stripping

½ teaspoon of ground cinnamon

2.5cm (1 inch) fresh ginger, peeled and chopped

1 teaspoon whole cloves

½ teaspoon crushed coriander seeds

150ml (¼ pint) water

225g (8oz) honey

150ml (¼ pint) brandy

1 With the exception of the honey and brandy, boil all the ingredients together until the berries are soft, then strain.

2 To each pint of juice add 225g (8oz) honey.

3 Simmer for 5 minutes.

4 Cool slightly and add 150ml (¼ pint) brandy to each pint bottle.

5 Add hot or cold water, as desired.

A soothing drink for colds and sore throats in winter.

Honeyed Pears with Mead

The defeat and slaughter of the Welsh at the Battle of Catraeth has been attributed, alas, to the mead they drank to excess before confronting the enemy. Little wonder then that those who adhere to the strict rules of Methodism consider the consumption of alcohol a sin. However, mead was exempt from this judgment since many rural families prepared it in time for the harvest. Honeycombs were steeped in cold water, which was then drained off and boiled. Hops and yeast were added during the process, prior to the mead being bottled in stone jars, which were often dug into the ground and left for at least six months before their contents were consumed.

1. Peel and cut the pears in half, remove their cores and chop the flesh into 2.5cm (1 inch) chunks.

2. Melt the butter in a pan, add the pears and cook for 7 – 8 minutes over a medium heat, tossing gently without breaking the fruit to a mush.

3. When the chunks are golden brown, pour over the mead.

4. Arrange the pears in a serving dish, dribble over the honey, dust with nutmeg and serve hot.

Ingredients

3 ripe pears

75g (3oz) unsalted butter

1 wine glass of mead

2 tablespoons runny honey

a pinch of freshly grated nutmeg

Welsh whi

According to legend, the distillation process was first brought to the shores of Wales by early Greek merchants in 365 AD, and on Bardsey, off the most westerly tip of the Llŷn peninsula, the process was adapted to distil ale and beer brewed by monks, who had established themselves on the island.

The essential ingredient of early brews was a mash of barley. It was fermented in the same way as beer but then distilled to make a spirit which the Welsh called *chwisgi*. In those early days, honey and herbs were added to the brew which was considered to be a pain killer and administered as medication, as well as an aphrodisiac.

After the dissolution of the monasteries by Henry VIII, distillation was carried on by farmers who used surplus grain from their harvests to prepare their various brews.

The first commercial distilleries in Wales were founded by the Evan Williams family of Dale in Pembrokeshire in the early 18th century, and the Daniels family of Cardigan, in the mid 18th century. Both families later emigrated to the USA to found the Kentucky Whiskey industry.

Almost a hundred years later in 1887, a distillery was established near Bala. It seems faintly ironic that at a time when the temperance movement was at its height in Wales, and in a town which was the centre of Calvinistic Methodism, someone should decide to open a distillery. However Mr R. J. Lloyd was keen for Wales to develop into a whisky distilling area, like the Scottish Highlands, and after testing water from various rivers in north Wales, Bala was chosen as the most suitable site, both for its water and for the fact that it was served by a railway. Under the guidance of a Scotsman, Mr Colville, the first whisky was produced in 1889. Bottles of Welsh whisky made their appearance with a painting of Jenny Jones in Welsh costume on the label. But alas, the venture was not a success.

With the closing of the distillery less than twenty years later, it was, perhaps, no loss, for the whisky was described as resembling hot, stagnant water, boiled for a week over a peaty fire! Perhaps it was only the fish who mourned the loss of the warm barley water which the distillery had so propitiously poured into the river.

All is not lost though with the production of whisky in Wales. At the turn of this century a group of friends set up a distillery in Penderyn, a small village in the Brecon Beacons. They commissioned a single copper pot still which produces alcohol of the highest strength. Matured in 2 types of barrels, Bourbon and Portuguese, the spirit is diluted with pure Breconshire water. The Penderyn Whisky company now create a fine range of whiskies but the limited production ensures that these products are rare and can be expensive.

Beer and c

Home brewing was very much part of Welsh rural life until the mid 19th century when the temperance movement effectively put a stop to the practice nationwide.

The barley was malted either at home on the farm, or in a local kiln, and home-made beer was traditionally served to workers at harvest time. A stronger brew was consumed at Christmas and particularly during some of the festivities which marked Old New Year's Day (*Dydd Calan Hen*). This tradition persists, for example, in the Gwaun valley in Pembrokeshire, a remote area that has, as yet, not succumbed to the temperance point of view!

Elsewhere in Wales, cider was the order of the day. According to J. Geraint Jenkins, author of *Life and Tradition in Rural Wales*:

Cider was widely drunk on the Welsh borders and in Breckonshire, so much so that in the nineteen thirties a certain Calvinistic Methodist preacher attending a sasiwn (preaching session) described Brecknock as 'a cider besotten county'.

Cider making usually took place on farms but often pubs had a cider house with an apple mill and a press. The apples from Golden Pippin, Redstreak, Kingston Black, Old Foxwhelp, Perthyre and Frederick were left on the trees in the autumn and then shaken to the ground and left to ferment for a couple of weeks. Often the stone cider mill was horse driven and once the apples were crushed into a pomace they were pressed to extract the juice.

J. Geraint Jenkins, *Life and Tradition in Rural Wales* (1976).

ider

Every household brewed its own beer which was a wholesome nourishing drink … On 19 July 1906, mother paid 5/6 for a bushel of malt and 1/3 for a pound of hops. There was usually several gallons left over after harvest, and although the beer would progressively become flatter, it was a fine drink, and when we were children we were allowed a spoonful of demerara to sweeten it. It was not only the family that enjoyed this home-brewed beverage, for after a brewing, the pigs were given the malt and the hops mixed in their swill and a dusting of barley meal, and we would occasionally witness the edifying spectacle of a pig who too much had taken, and was so high, that dignified progress was impossible through frequently collapsing on to its hind quarters to the accompaniment of unmistakable porcine laughter.

James Williams, *Give Me Yesterday* (1971).

Wild Wales

Grilled Mackerel with Lovage

15

wild wa

Wild Wales is ripe for picking. In summer and early autumn you can gather samphire on the shore or whinberries in the hills, watch Welsh families collecting laver off the rocks along the Gower and Pembrokeshire coast, scratch for cockles, gather mussels, pluck wild garlic from the woodlands and pick blackberries from unpolluted hedgerows.

B ut there is a much more serious side to gathering. There were times when jam-making and pickling fruit was a vital part of rural life, an insurance against running short of food during the winter months.

The Welsh have probably been using herbs in medicine since 1,000 BC: priests and teachers, or *gwyddoniaid* as they were known, used a variety of wild herbs to cure the sick. Later, during the 13th century, a collection of medical recipes was compiled by the physicians of Myddfai, Carmarthenshire. These physicians, according to legend and folklore, acquired their healing skills centuries earlier, through magic.

More recently, apothecaries would despatch herb gatherers to collect healing herbs from the countryside. Some herbs are very much part of the Welsh kitchen: for example, savory, a vital ingredient in faggots; wild thyme; marjoram; tansy and rosemary, used in powder form to flavour a cake. And flowers such as elderberries, clover, marigolds, nasturtium and violets have also been incorporated in Welsh dishes; sometimes to add flavour but more often than not to bring some colour to country cooking.

I once met a man who could remember taking a dried herring to school every day during the winter for lunch. He had been brought up in Cardigan and the herring harvest from the migrating shoals found along the coast during the autumn kept his family, and many others, in fish for the winter. Once caught, cleaned and gutted, the herrings would be hung in the chimney to dry. In the autumn, in days gone by, many people would buy a 'meise' of herrings, which amounted to about five hundred fish. The herrings were not washed, but simply layered in a cask with salt, and kept in a cool, dark place for a couple of months. When needed for the table, the fish were soaked in cold water overnight and then hung in the chimney to smoke.

Discovering samphire for the first time is a treat. Sometimes called sea asparagus, it grows on coastal marshes and mud flats. It looks like grass from afar but, on closer inspection, samphire has a thick stem with small nodules along its length. It grows to about 5cm (two inches) high and is a translucent, bright-green colour. The best samphire is that which is washed by two tides a day, and it should be gathered at low tide and eaten immediately. It will crunch in your mouth with a sweet, yet salty flavour. Samphire gatherers take bundles home and cook it simply by steaming or boiling, before serving with a dash of butter and black pepper. The crisp green tips can be used just as they are or in a salad.

Samphire makes a great addition to any fish dish or is delicious as a vegetable, served on its own.

Seakale grows around the Welsh coast, and particularly on rocks along the Pembrokeshire coast. The Romans made good use of seakale by preserving it in barrels; a food store for long voyages. The best and most succulent parts of seakale are the young flower heads, before they bloom. It is prepared like cabbage, boiled for a short time and eaten while still crunchy with a knob of butter and a grind of black pepper. Alternatively, seakale can be treated like cauliflower and baked with a creamy, cheese sauce.

Samphire and Seakale

Grilled Mackerel with Lovage

and Cracked Wheat Salad

A useful herb, lovage, but its strong celery flavour can all too easily dominate a dish. Mackerel can certainly hold its own, though, and I think that the marriage of lovage with this rich, oily fish is great. Straight from the sea, that's how mackerel should be eaten but if you do buy from a fishmonger, always insist upon fresh fish.

1 Fill the cavity of the mackerel with the sprigs of lovage, and arrange the fish in a grill pan. (You may have to cook two at a time if your grill pan is small.)

2 Squeeze over the lemon juice and season well.

3 Pre-heat the grill to its hottest setting, then cook the fish for about 4 – 5 minutes on each side.

4 The skin should be crisp and the flesh tender and moist.

Ingredients

4 plump mackerel, about 20cm (8 inch) long, cleaned

juice of 1 lemon

a good sprig of lovage for each fish

salt and freshly ground black pepper

---

1 To prepare the cracked wheat salad, cover the bulgar wheat with warm water and leave for 10 minutes.

2 Boil to soften, if needed (check the instructions on the packet).

3 Mix the herbs in a salad bowl with the lemon juice, olive oil, seasoning and spring onions.

4 Drain the bulgar well and sprinkle the grains into the salad bowl.

5 Toss the salad well before serving.

Cracked Wheat Salad

175g (6oz) cracked wheat (sometimes called bulgar or *pourgouri*)

a good handful of flat leaf parsley, finely chopped

25g (1oz) fresh mint, finely chopped

juice of 2 lemons

2 tablespoons olive oil

salt

freshly ground black pepper

4 small spring onions, trimmed and diced

Sorrel Soup with Goat's Cheese Croutes

Ingredients

450g (1lb) freshly picked sorrel

40g (1½oz) butter

1 small onion, diced

2 medium potatoes, peeled and cut into chunks

850ml (1½ pints) vegetable stock

4 slices of French bread

50g (2oz) fresh goat's cheese

Serves 4

1 In a large pan, melt the butter and cook the onion gently until soft.

2 Add the potatoes, stir well until covered in butter, then add the sorrel and stock.

3 Bring the soup to the boil and simmer gently for 20 minutes.

4 Cool, then liquidise or blend until smooth.

5 Toast the French bread on one side, turn over and spread the soft bread with goat's cheese. Toast until the cheese is brown and crisp.

6 Season the soup to taste, pour into bowls and float a crouton on top of each bowl. Serve immediately.

Season the soup to taste, pour into bowls and float a crouton on top of each bowl.

Ramsons Salad

Wild garlic, or ramsons, is found growing in profusion in damp woods and lanes the length and breadth of Wales. For most of the year you would hardly know they were there but during the spring, when the pretty white flowers are in bloom, the plant gives off a pleasant, mild garlic aroma. Simply driving along a country lane or walking through a wood you soon become aware of the garlicky smell wafting all around you. Ramsons are a very mild form of garlic and they make an ideal addition to salads and garnishes. Snipped into butter at the last minute, this herb adds just a hint of flavour, not as strong as the garlic bulb, but enough to cut into the richness of the dressing.

1. Arrange the lettuce in a large salad bowl.

2. Add the bacon, avocado and nuts.

3. Sprinkle over the fresh herbs and lastly, snip the ramsons over the top.

4. Mix and shake the ingredients for the dressing, and toss the salad well.

Ingredients

a good handful of ramsons, picked at the last minute

1 soft lettuce (lambs, oakleaf, curly endive, *lollo rosso* or *bianco*)

a good handful of mild fresh herbs, such as parsley and marjoram

8 rashers bacon, cooked and snipped small

2 ripe avocados, peeled and diced

1 tablespoon pine nuts or sunflower seeds

Serves 4

For the dressing

3 tablespoons best olive oil

1 tablespoon white wine or cider vinegar

1 teaspoon honey

1 teaspoon wholegrain mustard

salt and pepper

Come the spring tides of March and April, a very strange phenomenon may be seen on the River Wye, just south of Whitebrook. Visit the riverbank mid afternoon and you will find arranged, in a neat row, the most extraordinary nets, shaped like an outsize lacrosse stick, with no one claiming ownership. Return at night and the banks are crowded with fishermen, and the Wye waters thrashing with silvery elvers. Very seasonal and depending on the phase of the moon, the same men return year after year, armed with a bucket, a lamp and two forked tealing sticks to await the shout of 'tide' when the elvers swim upstream with the help of the rush of water.

Breeding in the Sargasso Sea, the tiny, almost transparent eels, no longer than 5 – 7cm (2 – 3 inches), travel across the Atlantic to swim up British rivers, where they spend the greater part of their lives before returning, when fully grown, to the Sargasso to breed.

The lower reaches of the Wye are tidal, and as the elvers swim alongside the banks on their journey inland, so the fishermen scoop them out with their antiquated-looking nets. All the fishermen hold licenses and while some return each year for the sport alone, many make a great deal of money exporting live elvers to Germany and Holland, where they are bred to full size for the benefit of all who enjoy smoked, jellied and pickled eel.

The tradition in Wales is to fry elvers for breakfast – a wonderful refreshing meal after a night beside the Wye. Indeed, elver eating competitions held in villages along the river banks are part of the tradition. The elvers are washed in running water and then cooked at once. As soon as the transparent mass touches the hot pan or fat, it turns opaque. The boneless elvers are stirred and turned until they are evenly cooked, and eaten with salt and pepper, and bread and butter.

Elvers

Gooseberry and Elderflower Sorbet

During warm summer months, when visitors to Wales enjoy pottering along the coast of Cardigan Bay, the simple summer flavours of gooseberry and elderflower refreshes the palate of a flagging potterer. This recipe, which makes about 1 litre of sorbet, was given to me by Sarah Holgate, who ran Hive on the Quay, an excellent watering hole in Aberaeron.

1 Wash the gooseberries and elderflowers and place in a pan with half of the water. Bring to the boil to soften, but do not leave to simmer, as this will deaden the flavour.

2 Cool and liquidise, strain through a nylon sieve and discard the seeds and skin.

3 Dissolve the sugar and honey in the remaining water, add the lemon juice, and mix with the fruit puree. Chill.

4 If using a freezer, pour the chilled mixture into a strong sandwich-type box to give a depth of approximately 3cm (1½ inches). Cover and place in the coldest part of the freezer. Check after 1½ hours.

5 A firm ring of ice should have formed around the sides and base of the box, with soft slush in the centre.

6 In a food processor, quickly process to a uniform slush, then return to the freezer in the same box. Repeat this process twice.

7 The sorbet will then need to be refrozen for a further 30 – 60 minutes.

8 If using an electric ice-cream machine, allow time to pre-chill the apparatus. Pour in the chilled syrup and churn for 15 – 20 minutes so that the sorbet becomes firm enough to serve, like softly whipped cream.

9 The sorbet is best served immediately.

Ingredients

250g (9oz) gooseberries (not tailed)

500ml (18fl oz) water, still mineral water if possible

65g (2½oz) granulated sugar

100g (4oz) clear honey, mild in flavour

juice of ½ lemon

3 large elderflower heads

Serves 4

Rhubarb and Gooseberry Jam

This is one of Lady Llanover's recipe

Ingredients

rhubarb and gooseberries

crystallised, moist sugar

1 Boil an equal quantity of diced rhubarb and gooseberries, that are not fully ripe, with three quarters of a pound of crystallised, moist sugar to one pound of fruit.

2 When boiled, it will make an excellent jam, similar to apricot.

When boiled, it will make an excellent jam, similar to apricot.

Gibbons Rolls

Gibbons, or spring onions, are a real favourite with south Walians, just as scallions are much loved in the north, and spring onions by the British in general. And, of course, they are all related to the leek. Gibbons, a perennial vegetable, are sometimes referred to as Welsh onions, and are grown in large bunches or clods.

I obtained this recipe from Lynda Kettle of Ty'n Rhos Country Hotel, near Bangor. Lynda has a particular skill for baking which is rarely surpassed – *good bakers are born not made*!

1. Pre-heat the oven to 425°F, (220°C), Gas 7.

2. Combine the flour and salt in a large mixing bowl and leave in a warm place for about 10 minutes.

3. Sprinkle in the yeast and sugar and stir well. (Fresh yeast must be mixed with a little water first.)

4. Pour in the water and mix to a firm dough.

5. Knead by hand or machine for 5 minutes.

6. Roll or pull the dough into a large rectangular shape, 60cm (2ft) long by 30cm (1ft) wide.

7. Sprinkle over the gibbons and parsley and roll up from the long side, like a Swiss roll.

8. With a sharp knife, cut the dough into sections or buns and stand them up on end.

9. Butter a baking sheet and place the buns fairly close together, so that they touch one another when risen.

10. Leave them to prove in a warm place for 30 minutes.

11. Brush the tops with milk and bake for 15 minutes in a hot oven.

Ingredients

1.5kg (3lbs) strong white and wholemeal flour, mixed

1 teaspoon salt

1 packet easy-blend yeast or 25g (1oz) fresh yeast

½ teaspoon brown sugar

100g (4oz) gibbons or spring onions, chopped green and white parts

1 tablespoon parsley, chopped

600ml (½ pints) warm water

25g (1oz) butter

Rowan, Crab Apple and Orange Jelly

From the time of the Druids, mountain ash has been regarded as a magic tree with strong powers over witches. Plant one near your door and, according to legend, you protect the house from evil. Sometimes rowan stumps are found in ancient burial grounds, and near stone circles where sacred rites were performed.

Used in cooking, the berries are sharp and sour, giving a superb flavour to preserves. In Wales, rowan jelly has a rightful place alongside Welsh roast lamb, for mountain ash trees are plentiful on the higher lands where mountain lambs are bred. The time to enjoy mountain lamb is late summer or early autumn, with a spoonful of rowan jelly made from the eye-catching, bright-red rowanberries which adorn the mountains during late August and September.

Ingredients

1.5kg (3lbs) rowanberries, picked over and washed

1.5kg (3lbs) crab apples, sliced

zest and juice of 3 oranges

light, soft brown sugar

a few drops of orange flower water

1 Place the berries, apples, zest and juice of the oranges in a saucepan and cover with water.

2 Simmer until pulpy, then strain through a jelly bag.

3 Measure the liquid and for every 600ml (1 pint) of juice add 450g (1lb) of soft brown sugar.

4 Dissolve the sugar slowly, stirring continuously, bring to the boil and boil hard until the setting point is reached.

5 Add the orange flower water.

6 Pour into clean, warm, dry jars and seal.

Whinberry and Apple Pie

A deciduous undershrub, whinberries are found on acid soils of heaths and moorlands. Whinberries flower from April to June and bear fruit from July to September. No one can ever put a price on time spent gathering food for free. In the past, one of the greatest treats of a summer's afternoon for townsfolk and country people alike was to gather the tiny, tasty wild berries from the Welsh hills and incorporate them in a pie. Whinberries are still gathered by energetic folk, and at the Nant Ddu Lodge, north of Merthyr Tydfil, visitors can tuck into whinberry pie. Whinberries to the Welsh, or wortleberries, blaeberries or bilberries elsewhere in the British Isles, but if you are unable to obtain them, then substitute with blackcurrants or blackberries.

1 To prepare the pastry, rub the fat into the flour until it looks like breadcrumbs, then stir in the sugar.

2 Add the egg yolk and enough cold water to make a firm dough.

3 Wrap in greaseproof paper and leave to rest in the fridge.

For the pastry

350g (12oz) plain flour

175g (6oz) butter and lard, mixed

100g (4oz) caster sugar

1 egg yolk

a few tablespoons cold water to mix

1 To prepare the filling, peel and slice the cooking apples and cook in a saucepan with the sugar, cinnamon and lemon juice. The apples should be soft, but ensure that they do not lose their shape. Leave to cool.

2 Roll the pastry and line a 20cm (8 inch) flan tin, reserving about a third for the pie lid.

3 Spoon in layers of apples and whinberries. Cover the pie with the lid, brush with cold water and sprinkle with sugar.

4 Bake at 375°F (190°C), Gas 5 for 25 minutes, or until golden brown.

5 Serve with fresh cream or a light custard.

For the filling

450g (1lb) fresh whinberries, picked over

5 large cooking apples

75g (3oz) caster sugar

pinch of cinnamon

juice of ½ lemon

caster sugar to glaze

Raspberry Vinegar

Fruit vinegars – sometimes in fashion, sometimes not – are easy to prepare and, during a hot summer, make a wonderfully refreshing drink, as well as adding a zip to all kinds of salads. Lady Llanover, in her indomitable way, suggested that making raspberry vinegar was an essential part of country life and should not be forgotten. This recipe has been gleaned from her writings.

1 Bruise 8 pounds of raspberries and pour on them three pints of good gooseberry or sugar vinegar.

2 Let them stand 24 hours, frequently stirring them with a wooden spoon.

3 Put 6 pounds of loaf sugar, broken in large lumps, into an earthen vessel, and the fruit and vinegar into a jelly-bag, wrung out in boiling water.

4 Let it drip upon the sugar till the juice is drained out, pressing it gently now and then.

5 Pour the liquor into a preserving-pan, and let it simmer until it boils up slowly over a moderate fire, and when cold bottle it.

A wonderfully refreshing drink, as well as adding a zip to all kinds of salads.

Elderberry Pickle

Bursting with juice and colour in the early autumn, elderberries have been put to good use in Wales for centuries. They make excellent pies, jams, jellies and cordials. Like other white-flowered, red-berried 'sacred' plants such as holly, rowan and hawthorn, elders are the subject of several superstitions. They are said never to be struck by lightening; that the weather never changes when they are in flower; that its wood is warmer than that of other trees, and that it is very imprudent to prune an elder after nightfall. If you have a self-sown elder growing in your garden, look after it; it's very lucky.

1 Wash the elderberries and drain thoroughly.

2 Sieve the berries, pressing out all the juice, to make a thin puree.

3 Place in a pan with the finely chopped onion and all other ingredients.

4 Bring to the boil and then simmer, stirring well, for 20 minutes.

Ingredients

675g (1½lbs) elderberries (weighed off the stems)

50g (2oz) light, soft brown sugar

½ teaspoon ground ginger

pinch of ground black pepper

pinch of ground cloves

1 medium onion, finely chopped

300ml (½ pint) cider vinegar

1 teaspoon salt

pinch of ground mace

50g (2oz) seedless raisins

Elderberry Sauce

for Vanilla Ice Cream

Ingredients

225g (8oz) elderberries

300ml (10fl oz) water

225g (8oz) sugar

good pinch of mixed spice

3 tablespoons port

whipped cream

1 Dissolve the sugar in the water and boil for 5 minutes, until syrupy.

2 Add the spice and elderberries, and simmer gently for about 10 minutes. Add the port and serve the sauce either hot or cold.

3 Scoop vanilla ice cream into a glass dish, pour over the elderberry sauce and top with a swirl of whipped cream. Serve with crisp biscuits.

Scoop vanilla ice cream into a glass dish, pour over the elderberry sauce and top with a swirl of whipped cream.

Elderflower Cordial

Elderflower may only grace our hedgerows for a few weeks each June but it is well worth making time to prepare some elderflower cordial to last throughout the year. Gather a basket of the freshest, largest heads of these fragrant, white, lacy flowers, before rather than after the rain, and prepare this simple cordial. It is an invaluable syrup to add to all kinds of fruit: delicious with strawberries; cooked with gooseberries; and perfect at the bottom of a trifle to add some fragrance to the sponge.

1 Place the citric acid and sugar in a saucepan with a little of the water and heat gently to dissolve.

2 Bring the rest of the water to the boil, pour it over the lemons and elderflowers and add the sugar and citric-acid solution.

3 Cover and leave in a cool place for 5 days, stirring well, morning and night.

4 Stir in the Camden tablet to sterilise the cordial and strain it into clean, dry bottles.

5 Store in a cool place. The recipe makes about 1.5 litres (2¾ pints) of cordial.

Ingredients

65g (2½oz) citric acid

2kg (4lbs) sugar

1.5 litres (2½ pints) water

2 lemons, sliced

20 heads of elderflower

¼ Camden tablet

Quince Paste

In mythology, the quince is the fruit of love, marriage and fertility. In spring time, the scent of flowering quince trees is inspirational, but it is not until autumn when the large, ugly-looking fruits appear and give us an opportunity to use their fragrance.

Ingredients

2kg (4½lb) quinces

300ml (½ pint) water

sugar to taste

juice of 1 lemon

1 Wash and cut the quinces. Place them in a large pan with the water. Bring to the boil and simmer gently until the fruit is tender.

2 Beat with a wooden spoon to break up the quinces and, when they are very soft, press them through a wire sieve.

3 Weigh the sieved puree and place it back in the rinsed pan with an equal amount of sugar.

4 Stir over a low heat until the sugar has dissolved, then add the lemon juice. Raise the heat and boil until the mixture thickens, candies and turns dark red. Stir continuously, but take care that the boiling puree doesn't spit and burn you.

5 When the paste is really thick, pour it into a shallow tin lined with greaseproof paper and spread it out with the aid of a spatula.

6 Place the tray in a warm place (an airing cupboard is ideal) and leave for a couple of days to dry.

7 Finally, cut the quince paste into squares and either serve it as it is or dust lightly with caster sugar.

The quince is the fruit of love, marriage and fertility.

Plum and Ginger Jam

1 Wash, quarter, skin and stone the plums.

2 Place the stones into a small pan with the water and boil for 10 minutes.

3 In a large preserving pan, place the plums and raisins, and the strained, stone liquid and simmer over a low heat until soft, stirring frequently.

4 Take the pan off the heat and stir in the warmed sugar until dissolved.

5 Bring to the boil and cook rapidly for 10 – 15 minutes until the setting point is reached.

6 Take the pan off the heat and add the ginger wine and ground ginger.

7 Leave to stand for five minutes before potting and sealing in the usual way.

Ingredients

1.75g (4lbs) plums

175g (6oz) seedless raisins

300ml (½ pint) spring water

1.5kg (3lbs) preserving sugar

4 tablespoons ginger wine

2 heaped teaspoons ground ginger

Autumn Fruit Chutney

1 In a very large pan, heat the vinegar with the onions and tomatoes.

2 Peel and chop the autumn fruit and add to the pan the sultanas, garlic and spice. Bring to the boil and simmer until the fruit and vegetables are cooked.

3 Add the sugar and continue to boil, without a lid, until the chutney has become thick and dark in colour. Bottle in the usual way.

Ingredients

1kg (2¼lbs) onions, peeled and chopped

1kg (2¼lbs) tomatoes, chopped

2kg (4½lbs) mixed autumn fruit (cooking apples, pears, plums, etc.)

450g (1lb) sultanas

2 cloves garlic, crushed with a teaspoon of salt

½ teaspoon mixed spice

½ teaspoon cayenne pepper

½ teaspoon ground mace

600ml (1 pint) pure malt vinegar

450g (1lb) demerara sugar

Index

L – P

Metric and imperial equivalents

Weights	Solid
15g	½oz
25g	1oz
40g	1½oz
50g	1¾oz
75g	2¾oz
100g	3½oz
125g	4½oz
150g	5½oz
175g	6oz
200g	7oz
250g	9oz
300g	10½oz
400g	14oz
500g	1lb 2oz
1kg	2lb 4oz
1.5kg	3lb 5oz
2kg	4lb 8oz
3kg	6lb 8oz

Volume	Liquid
15ml	½ floz
30ml	1 floz
50ml	2 floz
100ml	3½ floz
125ml	4 floz
150ml	5 floz (¼ pint)
200ml	7 floz
250ml	9 floz
300ml	10 floz (½ pint)
400ml	14 floz
450ml	16 floz
500ml	18 floz
600ml	1 pint (20 floz)
1 litre	1¾ pints
1.2 litre	2 pints
1.5 litre	2¾ pints
2 litres	3½ pints
3 litres	5¼ pints

Graffeg books

Seashore Safaris
Flavours of Wales
Rivers of Wales
Discovering Welsh Harbours
London Oyster Guide
Food Wales – eating out guide
Senedd
My Ryder Cup – the longest
  weekend
Market Town Wales
Caldey Island
Discovering Welsh Houses
Discovering Welsh Gardens
Pembrokeshire
Golf Wales

Bryan Webb's Kitchen
Food Wales
Celtic Cuisine
Skomer
Coastline Wales Arfordir Cymru
Landscape Wales Tirlun Cymru
Pocket Wales series
Village Wales
About Wales
About South East Wales
About South West Wales
About Mid Wales
About North Wales
Welsh National Opera

Graffeg
Tel: +44 (0)29 2078 5156
Radnor Court,
256 Cowbridge Road East,
Cardiff CF5 1GZ Wales
United Kingdom
sales@graffeg.com
www.graffeg.com

Graffeg books are available for
tablets, readers and mobiles
www.graffeg.com